About the Author

Michael Burt is a retired senior civil servant and an amateur historian. He is chairman of the Cowfold Village History Society and chairman of the Horsham District Heritage Forum. He has a particular interest in how national and international events affect the lives of ordinary people.

WHEN THE LIGHTS GO ON AGAIN

The story of Cowfold in World War 2

Michael Burt

Matador
9 Priory Business Park,
Wistow Road, Kibworth Beauchamp,
Leicestershire. LE8 0RX
Tel: 0116 279 2299
Email: books@troubador.co.uk
Web: www.troubador.co.uk/matador
Twitter: @matadorbooks

ISBN 978 183859 243 1

British Library Cataloguing in Publication Data.
A catalogue record for this book is available from the British Library.

Printed and bound by CPI Group (UK) Ltd, Croydon, CR0 4YY
Typeset in 11pt Adobe Garamond Pro by Troubador Publishing Ltd, Leicester, UK

Matador is an imprint of Troubador Publishing Ltd

History is recounted through the story told by unnoticed witnesses and participants. But the narrators are not only witnesses – least of all are they witnesses; they are actors and makers. It is impossible to go right up to reality. Between us and reality are our feelings. I understand that I am dealing with versions, that each person has a version, and it is from them, from their plurality and their intersections, that the image of the time and the people living in it is born.

Extract from *"The Unwomanly Face of War"*
by Svetlana Alexievich

Dedication

This book is dedicated to all the villagers and children of Cowfold and its surrounding area who lived through six years of war, enduring hardship and deprivation in a spirit of togetherness, courage and resilience the strength of which enabled them to persevere to the end. These are the unsung heroes who in their own quiet way contributed greatly to the final success, part of whose story is now being told.

The book is also dedicated especially to the memory of Bob Farren who lived in the village for nearly all of the 91 years of his life and who sadly passed away in February 2017.

Contents

Introduction   ix

The Children   1

The Village   8

The School   19

Who do you think you are kidding, Mr Hitler? 1939-1940   33

Keep calm and carry on! 1941-1942   81

The Canadians 1940-1943   97

The tide turns 1943-1944   104

The lights go on again 1944-1945   122

Acknowledgements   139

Appendix A: The 1939 Register   *141*
Appendix B: Maps of Cowfold village in 1939   *183*
Appendix C: The skies over Cowfold during WW2   *189*
Appendix D: Wartime recipes   *207*

Introduction

When the lights go on again all over the world
And the boys are home again all over the world
And rain or snow is all that may fall from the skies above
A kiss won't mean "Goodbye" but "Hello to love"

When the lights go on again all over the world
And the ships will sail again all over the world
Then we'll have time for things like wedding rings and free
    hearts will sing
When the lights go on again all over the world

This song, written by Bennie Benjamin, Sol Marcus and Eddie Seiler, was released in 1943 and was one of the memorable songs recorded by Vera Lynn, among other celebrity singers. Because of all the anxiety and fear caused during this time, the people needed an outlet, and that outlet came often in the form of hopeful songs. *"When the Lights Go On Again"* speaks of the hopes and yearning for an end to the war with its blackout and rationing restrictions, hopes that would seem far away at the time to people who were undergoing the stresses of being under attack. For many who heard the song, the title and lyrics also recalled the words attributed to Sir Edward Grey on the eve of the First World War: *"The lamps are going out all over Europe. We shall not see them lit again in our life-time"*.

This song, along with other memorable morale boosters and messages of hope such as *"Tomorrow is a lovely day"*, *"The White Cliffs of Dover"*, and *"We'll meet again"* would have been heard and sung by the villagers of Cowfold as they struggled to maintain as normal an existence as possible during the dark years of the war before the tide turned in favour of the Allies, and during the hardships imposed by rationing and blackout.

Because maintaining morale and as normal an existence as possible was what the villagers were determined to do whether at home or in the shops, in the streets, in school or in the fields. Maintaining civilian morale was a perpetual worry for the policy makers and authorities at national and local level. One definition of morale was provided by the social research organisation, Mass Observation, in 1941:

> *"By morale, we mean primarily not only determination to carry on, but also determination to carry on with the utmost energy, a determination based on a realisation of the facts of life and with it a readiness for many minor and some major sacrifices, including, if necessary, the sacrifice of life itself. Good morale means hard and persistent work, means optimum production, maximum unity, reasonable awareness of the true situation, and absence of complacency and confidence which are not based on fact".*

The villagers of Cowfold would have readily recognised this definition. The war saw many acts of bravery and heroism by the soldiers, airmen and sailors in the front line of conflict in the many theatres of the war, but equally true is the bravery, resilience and sheer determination to survive that were exhibited daily and for the six years of war by the men, women and children of communities across the country, of which Cowfold village was just one.

Does this make those villagers heroes? Heroism can be difficult to define and can mean different things to different people. There are many examples that one could use of bravery, fortitude and self-sacrifice to define heroism which have been exhibited in battle situations where often the term heroism is used (and one thinks here, for example, of soldiers who have been awarded the Victoria Cross). But heroism is not confined to battle. An interpretation of a hero is someone who puts other people's needs first, whether a neighbour or a member of the family. It is about meeting and overcoming challenges all the while not losing faith in oneself and one's ability to respond positively to whatever obstacle is put in the way. It is about courage, fortitude and the ability to carry on despite danger and hardships. And in the context of a village facing the danger of war, it is about trying to lead as normal a life as possible despite that danger.

This book tells the story of life in and around Cowfold, set against the backcloth of the momentous years of 1939 to 1945, largely through the eyes and memories of eleven children who lived in the area, with ages during the war ranging from under five to teenager. We are very privileged to be able to read their stories and in their own words.

There are very few stories here of bloodshed, death and destruction - Cowfold itself was never bombed and none of the villagers was killed by bombing. But there are stories here of making do with often very little, of life under the restrictions of blackout and rationing, of children's often wide-eyed excitement at watching the vapour trails of fighter aircraft battling each other in the sky; or even at rushing to the site of a crashed German bomber in the hope of picking up souvenirs. There are stories too of fear and dread at hearing the night-time throbbing engines of German bombers on their way to blitz London or returning and dumping unused bombs in the countryside around the village, or later the staccato sound of the Doodlebug's engine and then silence as the engine cut out followed by the destructive explosion. And for many as a backcloth to all this, the heart-wrenching goodbye and then constant worry for the safety of husbands, fathers or sons and daughters who were serving overseas or away from the village, news of whom came only infrequently.

For those who spent the war in their home village, town or city, this was their front line – the Home Front – where achieving victory in farming the fields or maintaining allotments as part of the Dig for Victory campaign, or just keeping calm and carrying on was no less important to the ultimate Victory than the battles that were fought on land, in the air and at sea.

And at the end it was left to Winston Churchill to speak for the nation on VE Day and to sum up what had been achieved:

"My dear friends, this is your hour. This is not victory of a party or of any class. It's a victory of the great British nation as a whole. We were the first, in this ancient island, to draw the sword against tyranny. After a while we were left all alone against the most tremendous military power that has been seen. We were all alone for a whole year.

There we stood, alone. Did anyone want to give in? Were we downhearted? The lights went out and the bombs came down. But every man, woman and child in the country had no thought of quitting the struggle. So we came back after long months from the jaws of death, out of the mouth of hell, while the world wondered "when shall the reputation and faith of this generation of English men and women fail"? I say that in the long years to come not only will the people of this island but of the world, wherever the bird of freedom chirps in human hearts, look back to what we've done and they will say "do not despair, do not yield to violence and tyranny, march straight forward and die if need be-unconquered".

Michael Burt
Shermanbury 2019

The Children

Bob Farren

Bob was born on 8th April 1926 in Worthing. He came to Cowfold probably after a week or ten days and lived at Sussex House, the white cottage now adjoining the Church lych-gate. He went to St Peter's School in 1931 when he was five and was there until 1940 when he went to Collyer's School in Horsham. While there he joined the Air Training Corps. He left Collyer's in 1944 and in July of that year enlisted in the RAF as a Leading Aircraftman Air Radar Mechanic. After initial training he was posted overseas for the rest of the war returning to Cowfold after VJ day in August 1945.

Pat Sawyer (nee Ferri)

Pat was born in May 1929 in London and came to Cowfold when she was three months old to live with her grandparents, William and Frances Bidwell, at Cotlands Cottages on the Horsham road

near to Homelands Farm (now a nursing home). Pat went to St Peter's School in 1934 and stayed there until 1943 when she was 14. After she left St Peter's, Pat worked in the Post Office in Cowfold for several years, which was run by Mr Humphrey, before joining the Post Office in Horsham where she worked as a GPO telephonist.

Mary Waller (nee Matthews)

Mary was born in February 1931 at Wilcox Farm, Kent Street and lived there throughout the war; she has lived on the farm since. The family have always farmed at that farm and in the area. Her father Mark was in the 8th Royal Sussex Regiment in WW1 and was awarded the Military Medal. Her father joined the Home Guard at the beginning of WW2 but left it full time after a short time to concentrate on running the farm. Mary went to St Peter's School in the Easter term of 1936 when she was five and left in 1945 when she was 14 to help her father on the farm.

Jean Ross and Barbara Temple (nee Ross)

Jean was born in December 1931 and her sister Barbara in June 1934. Both were born in a bungalow in the Bolney Road, Cowfold, called "Marlow". The bungalow belonged to Mr Dixon, one of Cowfold's butchers, for whom their father worked as a journeyman. From 1937 to 1946 the family lived in a flat above the garage at Longhouse off Picts Lane and their father worked as a chauffeur to Lady Barker who owned the "big" house. Their

father was called up in 1940 and joined the Royal Sussex Regiment with whom he served until he was demobbed in 1945. He was with the regiment at the siege of Tobruk and afterwards as part of the army of occupation in Palestine, Iraq, Iran and Syria. Jean went to St Peter's School in 1937 and Barbara joined her there in 1938. After St Peter's Jean went to Horsham High School in 1942 and Barbara followed her in 1944, both on a scholarship.

Jean Newton (nee Parsons)

Jean was born in 1933 in Barrack Cottages, Wineham. By 1938, when Jean went to St Peter's School, the family had moved to Church Terrace, Cowfold and she lived there through the war. Her father worked for the Council and was too old to join up when war was declared. He did however join the Cowfold Home Guard and served with them through the war. Jean left St Peter's School in 1948 when she was 15.

Elizabeth Arthur (nee Chase)

Elizabeth was born in 1935 in Horsham. She lived with her grandparents at "Chalfield" in Shermanbury. She was initially taught by a local governess but then was sent to boarding school in Devon in 1942/3. She was there until 1949 but came home for the holidays. Elizabeth's wartime memories are mainly of the area around Cowfold in particular Henfield, although the family did use Mr Goacher, the butcher and Wests the bakers, both in Cowfold and Mr Hodgson at Brook Hill Farm just outside Cowfold used to deliver milk to the family. Elizabeth's grandfather was a Lieutenant Colonel in the Shermanbury Home Guard. Elizabeth has recorded her wartime memories in her booklet "Recollections of Shermanbury... and more" extracts from which she has given permission to be used in this book.

Eric Vincent

Eric was born in Cowfold in 1936 in a house between Margaret Cottages and Mr Humphrey's Post Office. The family moved to Gloucestershire in 1937 where Eric's sister was born but returned to Cowfold just after the outbreak of war and lived with Eric's grandparents at No 1 Council Cottages on Station Road- which they called No 1 Station Road because that sounded better. Eric's father was a chauffeur and was called up in 1940 joining the RAF as a road transport driver. He was posted to Burma and drove16 ft trailers which were used to pick up crashed aircraft. Eric went to St Peter's School in September 1941 when he was five and stayed until 1951 when he was 15.

Colin Rudling

Colin was born in 1937 in London and moved to Woodside Close in Shermanbury just before the start of war. He went to St Peter's School in 1941and was there until 1949 when he went to Collyer's School in Horsham. Colin's father initially worked as a plumber for Fowlers but as this was a reserved occupation and he was not able to enlist, he left to become a gardener at Clock House and was then called up. He joined the Royal Electrical Mechanical Engineers and served with the 8th Army in Africa and Italy

Jim Parsons

Jim was born on 29 September 1939, 26 days after war with Germany was declared, at 20 Mill Lane, Lower Beeding and lived there through the war. His maternal grandmother lived in a flat above the Reading Room in Station Road, Cowfold. His father was a foreman at a market garden in Albourne which was a reserved occupation so he did not have to join up.

However he did join the Lower Beeding Home Guard. Jim went to St Peter's School in 1944 and stayed until 1951 when he went to Collyer's School in Horsham.

The Reverend Pat Sinton (nee Sayers)

Pat was born in 1941 at the Henfield Nursing Home. She is the daughter of Bert Sayers, then a well-known member of the Cowfold community. During the war she and her mother lived in a flat in Thornden House where her father worked as a chauffeur for the Cubitt family. He was called up in September 1939 and joined the Medical Corps. He was posted to North Africa where he worked on the provision of hospital beds and drove vehicles. Pat went to St Peter's School in 1945 and stayed there until 1952 when she went to Steyning Grammar School.

In addition the memories of the following people have been used:

Eileen Martin (nee Belton)

Eileen was born on 20th November 1918, the third daughter of Charles and Gertrude Belton; he was a qualified blacksmith. She lived with the family initially at Five Oaks, West Sussex before moving to West Chiltington in 1924 when she was six, and then to West Grinstead and finally to Cowfold where the family stayed initially in a two bedroomed house and then after another two years moved to 3 Oakfield Cottages on the Bolney Road. Eileen went to St Peter's School leaving in 1932 when she was fourteen. She initially was employed as a kitchen maid at Longhouse for two years before moving as a kitchen maid to the Lovett-Camerons at Brookhill House where she stayed until 1940 before getting a job as a cook at a house in West Grinstead; after a year she was employed as a cook at Allfreys along the Bolney Road. She married in August 1941 and lived with her in-laws in Partridge Green and worked for an engineering company in Horsham until after the end of the war.

Jessica Hawes (nee Buxton)

Jessica was born in August 1927 and was the seventh child and only daughter of Gordon and Mary Buxton. When Jessica was born the family lived at Laurel Dene (subsequently re-named Barrington Cottage) but they left there when she was three and moved to Stonefield Cottages. Gordon Buxton was employed as a chauffeur. Gordon Buxton had served in WW1 and in 1915 was "soldier servant" (batman?) to Lieutenant Colonel Edward Hermon who commanded the 27th Battalion of the Northumberland Fusiliers. Lieutenant Colonel Harmon was killed on 9th April 1917 during the battle of Arras and Gordon Buxton carried his body from the field. Jessica went to St Peter's School in 1932 and left in 1939 to go to St Christopher's School in Horsham. In 1940 she was sent by her parents to a boarding school outside Shrewsbury, but came home to Cowfold during the holidays.

The Village

How do you determine when a small ancient village like Cowfold came into being? What was its beginning? Was it at some unknown date when Anglo-Saxon herdsmen brought their animals through the forest, decided to pasture them in a clearing and gradually established a small community? Was it at some unrecorded time when a timber church was likely to have been built on the site of the present St Peter's Church? The short answer is that we do not know and probably never will know unless some undiscovered document turns up which gives us a better approximation of a start date. What we do know is that the village and its surrounding area are at least over 800 years old and that as with most old villages Cowfold evolved gradually and as a result of many influences.

But the story of the village, like any story of a life, does have key moments and events when it is possible to take a snap shot record of what the village was like, how and where its inhabitants lived, where they shopped and spent their leisure, where they went to school and where they worked. One such moment is on a Sunday morning in the late summer of 1939.

Sunday 3rd September 1939 was a warm sunny day in the South East with a temperature reaching into the 80 degrees Farenheit as the day wore on. Drawing back their curtains in the morning the people of Cowfold looked onto a benign and welcoming village basking gently in the sunlight and many were keen to get out of doors about their various early day tasks before the bells of St Peter's Church called them to the morning service. To all intents and purposes it was a normal Sunday morning in a normal, quiet Sussex village. And out at Wilcock's Farm, Kent Street, Mark Matthews would have been up since early morning milking his herd of a dozen Guernsey cows- a normal routine in the busy farming day.

But this was not a normal day and by eleven o'clock that morning the villagers' worst fears were confirmed and Britain was plunged once again into a cataclysmic World War with Germany, only 20 years after the end of World War 1, the so-called "war to end all wars". Little did the Farren family living in Sussex House, or the Reverend William Sandberg and his wife Ethel living at The Vicarage or Alfred and Edith West running the bakery on the Henfield Road or the Cubitt family living at Thornden, realise how much their lives and the life of the village would be changed by the next six years and by the years that followed.

So let me take that snap shot and imagine having a walk around the village at 9 o'clock on that sunny Sunday morning in the company of thirteen year old Bob Farren, whose father runs the garage in The Street next to the Red Lion Hotel, and ten year old Pat Ferri, who lives with her grandparents at "Cotlands" on the Horsham road. And here is what I discover.

Cowfold in 1939 is much the same self-sufficient village as existed in the years after the First World War apart from a few life changing introductions such as electricity which came into the middle of the village in 1927, piped water in 1938 and an automatic telephone exchange which was put in by the GPO in the same year. St Peter's Church, the Village Hall, the Red Lion Hotel and St Peter's School continue to be the main focal points of village life. In 1911 the village population was just over 1,000 and it is still about the same. The predominant occupation remains agriculture but a range of other trades are flourishing including saddlery, blacksmithing, tailoring, butchers and bakers, general stores (Sprinks' and Peacocks) and haberdashery. Fowler Brothers, whose business was established in the village in 1853, employs a sizeable number of men on building, blacksmithing, plumbing, house decorating and carpentry work; and they are also the village undertakers. The villagers can buy a wide range of food and other goods that have either been produced locally or brought in so there is little need for them to travel outside of the village for their shopping. For the children, sweets, which had been a luxury before the First World War, are now more available and in different varieties: Snickers were introduced in 1930, Mars Bars in 1932, Aero bars and Kit Kats in 1935, Maltesers and Blue Riband in 1936 and Smarties and Rollos in 1937.

Walking by the church lych-gate, built on the site of the old Forge, I meet Bob Farren who lives just around the corner in the white building known as Sussex House. Leaning on his newly acquired bicycle, bought for 12/6d, he tells me about the village:

"We have two of everything in the village- two general stores, Sprinks and Peacocks, two butchers- Mr Goacher and Mr Dixon, and two bakers- Mr Oliver on the Bolney road and Mr West on the Henfield road. My family runs the garage in the Street in Cowfold; a second garage- the Bridge Garage on the Henfield road is run by Dudley Tidy. We have five petrol pumps and sell some cars and sell and maintain bicycles. Because the garage has a charging plant for car batteries, we also charge up the accumulators and dry batteries for radios- they usually need to be charged once a week. We also sell wireless and torch batteries and electric light bulbs at Sussex House where I live.

The post office in Station Road is run by Mr Humphrey and he also sells all sorts of things, including boots and shoes. He has two daughters; Bessie who helps in the shop and Millie who runs the house and does the cooking. Just up the road from them is Mr Butcher who repairs shoes. Further along Station Road is Mr Ireland the saddler; his shop is at the entrance of the lane to St Peter's School.

A fishmonger comes to the village once a week by van – Mr Head from Horsham. We call him "Fishy Head". As a Saturday or Sunday treat, Mother sometimes buys winkles from him and at tea time we sit at the table with our pins hooking the winkles out and eating them.

There are various clubs in the village– football, cricket, stoolball, as well as institutions like the WI. The Village Hall is a centre of life along with the Red Lion and the church. So there is a sense of community about the village.

We don't have a great deal of traffic through the village. Most people walk or ride bicycles. But there's a No 17 bus service that runs from Horsham to Brighton; occasionally I will be dragged into Horsham with my mother when she wants to go shopping and then we take that bus. There is also a No 81 service running from Haywards Heath to Billingshurst. There's the odd car that comes through the village and uses my father's garage but cars are a bit of a rarity. I can remember a couple of years ago my mother taking my sister and me for a walk as far as West Grinstead station and having got that far going onto the platform and putting tuppence in the slot for a bit of Fry's chocolate cream before walking back. And I remember during that walk my mother stopping and saying "Hark, I think I can hear a car coming".

Sheep, cattle and horses are occasionally driven through the village to the farms around the area; I'm not sure where the horses would have been going but they come by train to West Grinstead station where Tommy Grantham is a horse dealer. Circuses and fairs with roundabouts and swing boats come to the village; it's very exciting when they turn up. I like to see the traction engines come through a five barred gate into the field behind the Red Lion, trailing their big trailers and caravans.

You can order things from Brighton and from Horsham and they will be delivered by bus. As well as getting fish from Fishy Head, people also order it from Horsham and it comes down on the bus. My father orders spare parts and things from the motor dealers in Brighton. The parcel drop off point is at our garage. Goods delivered to West Grinstead station are notified by card.

There aren't many people who have a telephone. We have one and its number is 44. That was before the automatic telephone exchange was put in and when Bessie Humphrey used to operate the manual exchange which was behind the counter in the post office along Station Road. She connected up people with whatever number they wanted- if it was anywhere outside the village it would be a long distance call! I think there was a fair chance that she knew everything that was going on in the village! When the automatic exchange arrived, a 2 was added to the front of the numbers so we are now 244.

The village doctors are Drs Sidney and Malcolm Dickens and Dr Matthews and the surgery is in a room at the side of Furzefield House where Dr Sidney Dickens lives. It's a waiting room cum dispensary and there's a consulting room in the house. I go up there occasionally to collect a medicine or something like that. If I am unwell, Mother usually calls Dr Matthews and he visits at our house; the doctors are on call 24 hours a day. A couple of years ago when I had been ill with something or other, he came in to see me and said I was getting on all right and he took me out on his rounds. Dr Sidney Dickens is the elder of the two and has a reputation for being "down to earth"- he is known to take *out some people's teeth without anaesthetic. Cuckfield hospital is where most routine operations are performed. Payment for the doctors is quite often via a Friendly Society if you are a member, from subscriptions some of which are kept as savings and some are put by for medical expenses.*

The district nurse is Nurse Baxter who has recently arrived in the village. She lives next to the Post Office in Station Road. She is quite a disciplinarian and you do what she says."

Bob pauses and then reflects on his home life:

"Mains drainage came into the village in the 1890s but in our house a bath consists of a tin tub and hot water heated on a stove. We don't have electricity although that came into the village a few years ago. Mother cooks on a two burner oil paraffin burning stove with an oven- a Valor oil stove- which stands on the top of it. This is basically a reasonable sized tin box with a door with a window so you can see through it, and a couple of shelves inside- it is amazing what she can cook on that. We always sit down to meals as a family. Father often has breakfast a bit earlier than the rest of us and we nearly always have a midday meal and more of a tea in the evening. We always have a roast for Sunday lunch/ dinner. Christmas dinner is always over at White Lined House with my grandparents when we have a goose. That's roasted in one of the small ovens like the one my mother has. It would have come from one of the local farms. We also have Christmas pudding with threepenny pieces in. As children we are also allowed a smidgen of port in a wine glass.

Mother sews by the light of an oil lamp and I have a small oil lamp to light my way to bed at night. We don't have any heating in the house except for an open fire which is lit only in one room, except maybe on Sundays when a fire is lit in the slightly larger front room. On one occasion when I was not well- it may have been measles or chicken pox- Mother lit a fire in my bedroom to warm it up but that was an exception."

Bob offers to show me around some of the village. As we leave the lych-gate and start to walk towards the Village Hall, we are joined by ten year old Pat Ferri who has walked into the village from her grandparents' home at "Cotlands" on the Horsham road. She's happy to share her thoughts about life in the village and confirms a lot of what Bob has been telling me. But she adds:

"The village has a thriving Young Farmers' Club, and, as Bob says, is a hive of industry with two butchers, two grocers, and two bakers. There are three postmen- William Shrubb, Bill Dale and William Sayers. Mr Sayers wears a leather protection on his arm which is permanently bent because of a World War 1 wound; he lives in No 4 Council Cottages on the Station Road.

Next door to Mr Humphrey's post office in Station Road, his sister May Humphrey has a drapers and sweet shop. Where we are passing now, St Peter's Cottage, is another sweet shop run by Mrs Welsh. A lot of us children are frightened of her and I'm not sure she likes us very much. There's a forge next to the Village Hall on the Bolney road which is run by Mr Charlie Belton, the blacksmith, and there's also a clock repairer who we call "Clockey Smith" who lives at No 1 Council Cottages at the West Grinstead end of Station Road; if you need to have a clock repaired you have to take it to him, he doesn't have a separate workshop. Also in Station Road is Fowler's carpentry shop but it's also the undertakers where coffins are made–there's always this loud thumping noise from the engine. There's also the Reading Room about half way down Station Road which is let out for functions and which has a flat above for the caretaker.

There are two carriers who serve the village; Mr Tidey at West Grinstead, who is also the coal merchant, and Mr King who lives at No 8 Council Cottages along Station Road. He has a lorry so uses that as a carrier. He also delivers the Sunday newspapers as distinct from the weekly ones. Then there is Ollie Crossfield who has a fairly large green van.

As Bob has said, we don't get much motor traffic through the village; mainly bikes and the occasional car or motorbike, but also horses and some livestock- sheep and cattle. I can play ball in the street on the way to school without the fear of being run over.

A Wall's ice cream man sometimes comes through the village on his bicycle selling ice-creams and you also sometimes see an AA man on a bicycle."

Pat adds some further information about the doctors:

"The doctors are Dr Sidney Dickens, who is the father, Dr Malcom Dickens who is his son and Dr Thomas Matthews. There is a surgery every day of the week including Sundays; morning and evening surgeries on Monday, Tuesday, Thursday, Friday and Saturday and just morning surgeries on Wednesday and Sunday. Dr Matthews reads the lesson at church and is often late because surgery has overrun!"

We walk past St Peter's Cottage and Sprinks' general stores, which has been serving the village since 1887, and cross the road to stand outside the Village Hall. This was erected by Fowlers but paid for and given to the village by that great friend and benefactor, Frederick Du Cane Godman in 1896 and became, and still is, one of the focal places of village life. Frank Muncey, the caretaker but also a member of the Police Reserve, is outside talking to a group of worried looking villagers. Looking across the road, in front of us is

Fowlers' main office and running along The Street, Farren's garage with its five petrol pumps, Arthur Dixon the butcher at Palmeston House immediately across the road from another butcher, James Goacher at Olde House, the Red Lion Hotel run by Robert Spinks and in the distance, Walter Peacock's general store at Jersey House. This is the heart of the village where the road from Bolney meets the road coming up from Henfield and together go north to the Red Lion Hotel where one branch heads along Station Road towards West Grinstead and the other goes directly north over Brook Hill towards Lower Beeding and Horsham; along that road is the doctors' surgery and Brook Hill House where the Lovett-Cameron family live and to the right the entrance and lodge house for the main house Thornden (previously called Hampsteel), the home of the Cubitt family.

To the left we look down the Henfield road. There, on the left, past Fowlers' transport yard, are the row of houses, many of which had been built by Fowlers, which lead down to the Hare and Hounds pub, to the Bridge Garage and to Cowfold Lodge, the home of Captain and Mrs Rookhurst-Roberts. Among those living in those houses are the Fowlers, the Slocombes, the Tindalls, the Harveys, the Langridges, the Shrubs and the Packhams. On the right are some of the older Cowfold houses – Church Farm House, a 17th century timber framed two bay house, the home of William and Alice Walder, and the 19th century Steyne House- which come before the newer houses including the police house occupied by Constable Albert Elliott, his wife Lilian, their daughter June and three year old son, David. Beyond that is the bakery run by Alfred and Edith West; he is also a special constable. Almost opposite the Hare and Hounds is the Noah's Ark café run by Sophia Gilson, and just beyond that the old Cowfold Grammar School, closed in about 1912; it is now a private house called Wood Grange occupied by Percy Maynard and his wife Lucy among others. From there the road heads out towards

St Hugh's Monastery, whose spire can be seen for miles around and whose Sancta Maria bell is a familiar and comforting sound for the villagers, and then on to Shermanbury and Henfield.

Because it's a Sunday the shops are closed. But the village at this point is busy with people going about various tasks before heading to St Peter's Church for Sunday service. 89 year old Billy Sprinks, the oldest Cowfold villager, is outside his general stores in his white apron sweeping the pavement in front of the shop; he waves us a cheery hello. A few children are playing ball in the dusty road already warming up with the promise of a hot day, safe to do so because of the lack of traffic. There isn't the level of noise or the movement of vehicles that a weekday brings. Fowlers' yard, a cacophony during the week, is quiet now. So is the thumping engine in Fowler's carpentry shop along Station Road. Instead there is the sound of people's footsteps and voices calling out morning greetings to neighbours and friends, or snatches of conversation from small knots of worried people who have gathered to discuss the impending war with Germany including those gathered outside the Village Hall; at least one note of defiance reaches us as someone utters that Sussex motto *"We wunt be druv"*. Another topic of conversation is the arrival only the day before of evacuees from London which have swelled the village population; most of these have been found homes with foster families but a few have still to be billeted. And on the air, there is the intermingled smell of someone's bacon and egg breakfast and of newly baked bread.

We turn and walk along the Bolney Road. A few houses down on the right is Charlie Belton's blacksmith shop, quiet now but still smelling of the coke used to fire the forge, and just beyond that, a lane to the right takes us past George Oliver's bakery. Further on there is the row of houses known as Huntscroft Gardens where among others live George and Mary Barton at Number 2 and Ted and Nellie Woolven at Number 1 and beyond those, the Oakfield cottages where Charlie Belton lives with neighbours including Albert and Nellie Minihane. Among other houses here there is Marlow, the home of George and Edith Constable, before the road leaves Cowfold for Bolney. Across from the Bolney road are the playing fields, let by the Godman family to the village in the early 1900s, and beyond those the woods known as Alley Groves, a favourite haunt of the village children for pond fishing, and further on Baker's Shaw spinney, full of periwinkles and bluebells in the early summer.

At that point I say goodbye to Bob and Pat and thank them for the tour and I watch them as they walk back along the road, Bob, wheeling his bike, to his home at Sussex House and Pat to her grandparents' home on the Horsham Road. As they turn the corner by the Village Hall they wave and then disappear.

As I walk back towards the Red Lion, I meet PC Albert Elliott. I ask him about his work in the village and surrounding area. He tells me that the village does not have much crime, usually petty offences but which nevertheless keep him busy. He tells me that during 1939 and to date there had been 10 simple and minor larcenies, 4 offences of obtaining goods by false pretences, 2 housebreakings, 2 thefts of unattended vehicles and 2 thefts of unattended bicycles. He is proud to tell me as well that nearly 95% of the offences had been detected and the perpetrators brought to justice. I congratulate him on that!

This then is the village on that doomed Sunday morning in September 1939. The normality of this quiet late summer morning masks the anxiety that most villagers have been feeling at the inexorable march towards war, despite the efforts of Neville Chamberlain to appease Hitler and the "Peace for our time" paper that he waved optimistically at Heston Airport nearly a year previously.

By eleven o'clock that morning their worst fears have been confirmed and six years of struggle, hardship and loss have begun.

The School

By 1939, St Peter's was the only school in Cowfold, the Grammar School on the Henfield Road having closed in about 1912. The school was built in the 1870s by a Mr Richard Hoper of Homelands on the site of Potter's House at Potter's Green at the West Grinstead end of Station Road, to replace the school which had been built by the vicar, Reverend Richard Constable, in 1813 on the Horsham Road opposite Brook Farm. St Peter's became a Church of England school in 1901.

In 1939 the school comprised one main building with accommodation for the headmaster, and a playground separated by a wall into a girls' and infants' side and a boys' side. There were segregated outside toilets. On the boys' side there was a wooden coal shed with an open front but with boards to keep the coal in. There were also separate bike sheds for the boys and girls.

In July that year, the school had 118 children with ages ranging from 4 or 5 to 14. The management of the school was overseen by a board, whose chairman was Colonel C.B. Godman (he retired as chairman in September 1939 after 36 years but continued to visit the school until his death on 18th January 1941, aged 92; he was succeeded as chairman of the managers by the Reverend W. B. Sandberg (vicar of St Peter's church)). The other managers were Captain Hodgson, Mrs Cameron, the Hon. Mrs C.G.Cubitt and Doctor Sidney Dickens. A great benefactor of the school was Dame Alice Godman until her death in October 1944.

Medical care for the school was provided by Dr Matthew Dickens and by Nurse Florence Baxter. The dentist was Mr Brabazon who visited from Horsham. The latter is well remembered by Colin Rudling:

> "Mr Brabazon was gruesome. I had to sit in the cloak room waiting to be called surrounded by several children who had had teeth out, some crying with mouths full of blood soaked in cotton wool. Luckily I didn't need any extractions but I did have a filling or two which was very painful. The drill was a cast-iron contraption which the dentist worked with his foot to get the speed up whilst grinding away at your teeth; it was a dreadful thing and there were no injections to kill the pain and when he hit the nerve, you certainly knew about it! It took me years to get over that."

The headmaster was the redoubtable Mr Reginald Quick who had been at the school since 1908 (and would remain as headmaster until his retirement in 1948). He was renowned as a very strict disciplinarian and a stickler for routine, and not surprisingly made a lasting impression, often negative, on the children. He has been described by Bert Sayers in his schoolboy memories of Cowfold and the school, as *"a tall well-built man with hands the size of plates it seemed"*. And this is confirmed by Barbara Ross who recalls: *"I can see his fingers now. They were very fat with very black hairs. His hands were enormous."* Jean Ross remembers Mr Quick always wore plus four trousers and knitted socks.

Others remember his discipline, which by today's standards would be deemed unacceptable if not unlawful although then was accepted as part of learning and growing up. Eric Vincent and Jean Parsons remember that "Quick the stick" as he was called by some *"could be quite vicious and cruel. He would creep up behind you. One day I saw him push a boy's head down onto the desk and he got a nose bleed."* Colin Rudling recalls that *"he wasn't a very nice person. He thumped me on the back once and I practically saw stars. He had no apparent sense of humour whatsoever, although he was getting old by then."* But Colin's biggest objection to Mr Quick was *"if you were left-handed as I was, he made you write right-handed. There was one boy, David Elliott, who was a year older than me, who was made to change to right-handed and he developed a dreadful stutter which people have said was caused by that."*

Hard work, routine and consistency were three by-words of Mr Quick's approach to education and life. That was reflected in the way he had run St Peter's School for the past 30 years and would continue to run it for a further ten years until his retirement in 1948. He was also a stickler for correctness in everything. Eric Vincent remembers him asking one day what Eric had had for dinner. *"Meat and plum puddin'* "I said and Mr Quick said "What was that? Plum puddin'? It's not plum puddin'." *So I got into trouble for not pronouncing pudding properly!"*

Corporal punishment was an accepted part of school education until it was outlawed in 1986 in state schools and private schools where at least part of the funding came from the Government and in other private schools in 1998. The justification for this was that teachers were considered authority figures granted with the same rights as parents to punish children in their care. So it was not just Mr Quick who meted out punishment which could be for a particular misdemeanour or for simply getting an answer wrong. Colin Rudling recalls: *"One of the teachers, Miss Sprague, had a ruler which she would flex and you never seemed to get through the day without* being rapped across the knuckles with her ruler often for no apparent reason although perhaps I deserved it! It was a permanent weapon on display." Colin also remembers a particular instance of a whole class being caned: "Caning was very frequent although sometimes you got the option between cane and lines and you would have needed to have done much to get either of those punishments. Sometimes if no-one owned up to something the whole class would be caned and that would have been a class of about 30. It happened once with Mr Slocombe because somebody-actually his son- put two drawing pins on his chair and he sat on them. He went puce with rage and of course we couldn't help laughing. He said unless someone owned up to this he would cane the lot of us; although it may just have been the boys. But anyway Brian (the son) didn't own up to it and nobody ratted on him, so we all got the cane." And a child could be the innocent recipient of a whack, as Jean Ross remembers: "I can remember when I was in Standard 1 – when I was just seven- Mr Slocombe came in to take us for geography and the boy behind us had been misbehaving. So Mr Slocombe said "Stand up. Put your hand out". So of course the boy put his hand out over my shoulder, the cane came down, missed the boy and hit me on the shoulder. I didn't really like Mr Slocombe after that! When later on he went into the Air Force and was fairly soon taken prisoner of war, I remember thinking "Oh good, he won't be back before I leave his class" and then feeling terribly guilty."

That the application of corporal punishment was so ingrained in the daily routine of schooling can be borne out by an incident remembered by Mary Matthews: "On one occasion the boys collected all of Mr Quick's canes together when he wasn't looking, broke them up, and put them in the big combustion stove in the other half of the assembly hall which was in Miss Archard's class. But it wasn't long after that he came in from his house carrying a big bundle of raspberry canes and said "It's all right boys I've got plenty more were these have come from".

Pat Ferri recalls that he "was a strict disciplinarian of the old kind and I didn't like him. He was of his time." But for all that, the school under Mr Quick did get good results and for some like Jean and Barbara Ross, very bright pupils, it was a happy experience. Jean recalls: *"We had a very good education at the village school. We were put through it; it was strict but I was happy"*.

The teachers below Mr Quick changed from time to time either because they moved to another school or retired or their contract expired. When Bob Farren went to the school in 1931 there were four classes of mixed boys and girls and only three teachers, including Mr Quick. He took the top class of twelve to fourteen year olds, he and Miss Kathleen Archard shared the class of ten to twelve year olds, Miss Archard took the class of seven to nine year olds, and Miss Evison took the infants' class of five to seven year olds. Pat Ferri who went to the school in 1934, remembers Miss Archard as *"very young and she used to take us down the fields and introduce us to various butterflies and other things"*. Miss Archard was 23 years old at that time.

By 1937 when Jean Ross went to the school, the teachers were Mr Quick, Mr Slocombe, Miss Archard and Miss Beakhouse who took the infants; Jean remembers Miss Archard wore air force blue knitted wool stockings.

In September 1939 the teachers were Mr Quick, Miss Archard, Mr Slocombe, Miss Sprague (who was a supply teacher) and Mrs Burdfield who took the infants and who had replaced Miss Evison. Mrs Burdfield resigned in October 1943 and her place was taken by Miss Joan Fisher; Colin Rudling remembers Miss Fisher as *"always smiling and in a cheery mood unlike some of the teachers who taught me later"*. In 1941 a Miss Tidy (an uncertified teacher) was appointed for the rest of the war period, probably to fill the gap left by Mr Slocombe who had enlisted in the RAF in October 1940, and her employment finished on 2nd August 1945.

Unlike today when many of the teachers travel in from some distance to the school- for example from East Grinstead and

Littlehampton- most of the teachers before and during the war lived locally. Mr Quick lived on site with his wife Rosalind and was therefore always at the school whatever the weather. Miss Beakhouse and Mr Slocombe lodged with the Irelands in the village, until he married when he and his wife Margaret lived at West View on the Henfield Road. Mrs Burdfield, Miss Fisher and Miss Tidy lived in Partridge Green. Miss Archard's home was in Sompting but she lodged with the Boxalls at Carleon on the Henfield Road near the Noah's Ark cafe.

Getting to and from the school was obviously not a problem for the children who lived in the village but for those living outside in Shermanbury, Lower Beeding, down Kent Street and at or near Longhouse off Picts Lane, this represented a challenge particularly during the winter. Some children were picked up and taken home by Mr Tidey the coal merchant who used his lorry to deliver coal and children. Barbara Ross remembers this well:

"Living at Longhouse we all had to walk down the lane to the main road at Oakendene crossroads. There were six families, the Packhams from Upper Bulls wood, the Cherrymans, us, the Capses, the Blakes and the Pages. We all gathered each other up and walked down to the crossroads where we had to wait for the school lorry. This was Mr Tidey's lorry- he was the coal merchant- a flat-bed lorry with a canvas roof and low sides with wooden benches on either side. He went down to Wineham first and picked up the children from there and then came along to pick us up. We did this in all weathers including when it had been snowing. Coming home if you saw two tracks in the snow you knew that Mum had been out with the pram."

"I can remember Mr Tidey getting out the wooden steps so we could climb into the back. At the back of the lorry there were waist-high sides with the rest open, so you were just trusted to sit there and behave yourself. No seat belts!"

It must have been freezing in winter!

Colin Rudling got to and from school by the No 17 bus which picked him up from the start of Woodside Close in Shermanbury and dropped him off at the Village Hall from where he walked to school. The fare was 2d. Jim Parsons recalls getting the No 17 bus with other children from Crabtree and being dropped off at the Village Hall. Going home he was picked up at Sprinks' Stores.

The school day started at 9 o'clock with Assembly with Prayers, followed by Scripture. For that the children who were Roman Catholics sat out in the lobby and re-joined their classmates afterwards. Jean Ross remembers that *"Mr Quick would come in and say "Good morning girls and boys" and we would say "Good morning Mr Quick" and salute. And then we had a psalm; there were two jumbo sized rolls of papers with psalms written on one side and hymns on the other. So we had a psalm, a prayer, a hymn and a bible reading."*

Scripture was followed by Arithmetic and English which took the day up to the mid-morning break and playtime when the children had a third of a pint of milk each. This was delivered by the Arun River Dairy Company and came in little bottles with a cardboard lid and a hole in the middle for a straw. Barbara Ross remembers using the lids to make pompoms. Colin Rudling recalls on one occasion *"a boy downing his milk only to find a large slug curled around the inside of the bottom of the bottle. How we all laughed and I'm sure that he actually turned green, although perhaps I'm imagining that bit."*

Colin also remembers that during that break, the boys played games such as conkers (in the season) and marbles. *"There was also a game called rather unimaginatively, "Running across". This started with one boy in the middle and all the others rushing from one corner of the playground to the opposite side; if the boy in the middle caught and held on to one of the runners then that boy had to join him in catching and this continued until there was just one runner left, who was then declared the winner. Many skinned knees were suffered playing that game!"* Another name for this game is *"British Bulldog".*

Lunch followed the milk and playtime break. The school did not have a canteen until after the war so those who lived in the village like Bob Farren walked home for lunch; those who lived outside the village like Jean and Barbara Ross, Colin Rudling and Pat Ferri brought packed lunches.

After lunch a few of the very young infants were able to have a rest for about an hour on little camp beds which had child sized green blankets. For everyone else (and the infants after their rest period) the afternoon comprised additional lessons such as History and Geography, Gardening, Art, Needlework (for the girls), Cookery (once a week on a Thursday) and Singing. Mr Quick took those singing lessons. Jean Ross recalls *"learning a classical song about trees, and to think that was being taught to nine year olds! I also remember the emphasis he put on words in the verses of Jerusalem-* **"Bring** *me my* **bow** *of* **burning** *gold"; he made us sing that time and time again."* Bob Farren also remembers that Mr Quick *"was rather keen on the children learning the Hallelulah Chorus. He did once organise an outing to the Albert Hall to a performance of Hiawatha, and I think we probably went by coach which might have been run by the Southdown Bus Company. His musical hero was Malcolm Sargeant also known as "Flash Harry".*

In addition the Reverend Sandberg came to the school once a week to give religious instruction. He was clearly not to everyone's taste as Colin Rudling remembers: *"Reverend Sandberg was a real hell and damnation vicar. All his sermons were about people going to hell if they didn't do such and such. He was the angriest man I have ever met. There was never a kind word from him, ever. I had confirmation classes with him and it was rather like the Spanish Inquisition! When the Bishop of Chichester came round and did the confirmation, I was amazed at how pleasant he was."*

Cookery lessons for the older girls were given sometimes in some old buildings which were part of Thornden House, and sometimes in the Old Reading Room on Station Road. Pat Ferri recalls: *"My grandmother was a great cook who had been trained in London by a French chef and she didn't approve of the cooking. But it was perfectly adequate. There was a paraffin stove that had burners; one or two burners were left free for boiling and two fed the heat for the oven. We used to have to prepare a hot meal for those school children whose parents were willing to pay- things like Cornish pasties, two vegetables and an adequate pudding. We also used to make cakes and certain people in the village were on a list and we used to go to their houses with trays of cakes and so on. During the war the school must have had a rationing allowance to allow this to happen. Nothing was wasted; burning or curdling was very rare."*

Mary Matthews also remembers: *"I also enjoyed going to cookery lessons. For those we used to have to go over to Peacock's shop to get our rations. I think when we made cakes, we could only make six so it must have been only an ounce of margarine and dried egg; we must have been able to get the flour. We had a strange stove with three paraffin burners underneath which used to feed the oven at the top- but it was quite efficient. We used to make lovely fairy cakes and things like that; occasionally we made pastry things. I also remember making brandy snaps, rolling them around the wooden spoon handle. I think we used to take what we made home with us but I can remember giving Mr Quick one of my fairy cakes!"*

The school day ended at 3.45 pm and all the children left at the same time, the village children walking home, some children being taken home by in Mr Tidey's lorry and others catching the bus north or south.

Among the notable dates in the school calendar was Empire Day, celebrated each year on the 24th May. In the 1920s this was a day for high patriotism when the children were drilled and taught to salute the Union Jack, and when in the company of the school managers, they sat through a patriotic speech from the headmaster, prayers and hymns and the presentation of a medal. In the run up to the outbreak of World War 2 and during the war, this had perhaps greater meaning and a greater poignancy for those children whose fathers or brothers were serving with the Forces.

But as for many such occasions, there was always a humorous side, as Barbara Ross recalls:

> *"When we had Empire Day we all used to go down to the Village Hall. We had to sing Jerusalem and other hymns standing on wooden portable steps that led up to the stage and Mr Quick would get up on the stage to conduct us and he would get so exuberant I was always waiting for him to topple over."*
>
> *"I remember having to wear red, white and blue ribbons. We used to get those from Miss Ireland, Bill Ireland the saddler's sister who ran the haberdashery shop as part of Sprinks' Store. There was a great big mahogany counter and all these ribbons were in trays underneath and the small things were over this side in a divider in the shop. So if you asked her for something out of the drawers on the divider, rather than her walking all the way round, she would sit on this counter, swing her legs over and then come down. Well we used to ask her just for something from the divider because she wore the most enormous bloomers so we did it just to see those!"*

The school also put on an annual concert which was held in the Village Hall. Barbara Ross remembers one concert in particular:

> *"I remember we were doing a concert in the Village Hall on one occasion and in our class there were twins, Sally and Judy Roe, who lived at Cooper's Cottage. The play was about fairies or something and there were two characters in it so Sally and Judy were the*

obvious choice for those parts. About a week before the concert, they went down with one of these infectious diseases so it was all panic in finding two replacements. So I was chosen as one and John Matthews from Wineham was the other one. My character was Phoebe. I can remember Mum coaching me at home with the script, her reading one part and me reading the part of Phoebe. It came to the performance and my teacher was Miss Hyatt. In one of the scenes I had to come onto the stage first and do a solo dance barefoot in some little tunic accompanied by Miss Hyatt on the piano. So I drifted around the stage and at the end of the dance, I had to sit down at the front of the stage while something else went on behind me. So I did that but to my mother's consternation I started looking between my toes. I can remember sitting there and thinking "Oh gosh I don't like doing this".

Outside of school hours and during the holidays, the children had almost complete freedom to roam the countryside. It is hard to imagine this now with so much emphasis placed on parents not letting their children out of sight; but then children were much wiser to what the countryside had to offer including its dangers.

Bob Farren remembers:

"After school a group of us would go out and play. I can remember several of us getting together and going down the Henfield road to Fowler's timber yard and playing in there. Nobody seemed to mind. We had a lot of freedom. We would go out and do more or less what we wanted to. We would go out preferably into the woods, play cowboys and Indians and things like that. We would go fishing and moorhen nesting. We'd also do a bit of collecting bird's eggs. We'd collect cigarette cards and swap them at school. I was 14 when I got a 12 bore shotgun and used to spend a lot of time at Crateman's Farm. I had the run of Crateman's Park,

Pooks and Oaklands and I would do a bit of rough shooting with a dog. We also used to go ferreting; my father had two ferrets and my sister used to exercise them in the field on a string attached to their collars. Our catch would be brought home for the pot and would also include pigeons.

I would also help with harvesting and haymaking at Crateman's farm. I remember in 1940 when Mr Thomas, the farmer, got his first Fordson's standard tractor with rubber tyres which was fitted with a sweep on the front for gathering up the hay and pushing it over to where it would be built up into a stack.

I didn't have a bicycle until I was probably thirteen which was bought for 12/6d. In 1940 my father bought both my sister and me a new bicycle because he said that if we were going to have a decent bicycle we had better have it then because it wouldn't be long before there was no chromium plate because of the war. Eventually I acquired a speedometer and with a friend who had a similar bike and a speedometer, we would cycle to the top of Crabtree hill and see how fast we could go coming down the hill. Of course the traffic wasn't anything like it is now and towards the end of 1940 it was much diminished".

Jean and Barbara Ross who lived at Longhouse recall:

"Outside of school and during the holidays we had different interests. If I (Jean) could, I would sit with a book and read. If it was me (Barbara) I was out of the door to the fields and woods. There was plenty of opportunity to play and meet up with the local children. We used to mix and match and we had different clubs. Each club would have a theme. I (Jean) can remember thinking up the Fungus club at one time and we would go off and collect fungi. I realise now that we learnt ecology on the hoof because if you went one way you found primroses and such like, and if you went up

the hill towards Bull's Wood where it was sandy, you would find bluebells and wild strawberries and things like that. The oak trees were down the other way. So we knew the area intimately.

We were allowed freedom to roam. We just used to say to Mum that we were going down to the daffodil wood and she would know exactly where we were going. There were two fields not far from the house where there was a very steep bank which was a rabbit warren. On top of that bank was a big oak tree with a bough which came right out, so you could get on the bough at the top and swing on that thinking that you were on a galleon. So we used to say we were going either down the primrose bank, or to the rhododendron wood, or down the steep path to the river.

Considering that this was during the war time we really had a considerable amount of freedom. I (Barbara) used to go up to North Farm, owned by Mr Benjamin Capsey, a lot and when it was hay making time he used to let us play with the hay in the long strips that were laying ready to be picked up and pitchforked onto the waggons. We used to help with that. And then we would get a ride on the top of the waggon back to the farmyard."

Living on a farm, Mary Matthews inevitably had to help although she did find time for play.

"After school and during the holidays I spent most of my time playing with a girl who lived in Barrack Cottages. We weren't allowed in the house, except perhaps if it was raining, so we were more or less outside from morning to night. As for bedroom, that was for sleeping in and you didn't go to that room until you went to bed for the night. We were given absolute freedom; we cycled everywhere and walked everywhere, met other children.

I think I got my first bicycle as soon as I was able to ride it- around five or six. I can remember riding on tiny little bikes from *here up to Plummer's Plain which was where my grandmother lived and we thought nothing of it. Of course there wasn't the traffic around at that time although during the war there was more traffic in the woods. Kent Street was made a one way traffic route. However we could still cycle around most places despite restrictions. Summer holidays were spent working on the farm. We never got paid to start with. But I can remember some children from the village got paid 3d an hour for working on the farm so in the end my Dad had to pay us!"*

What was about to break over the children's heads would have a memorable impact on their lives at the time but for most the war years seem to have been a time of quite some excitement interspersed with the odd moment of fear. The children adapted as much as possible to the changed circumstances of their life but they carried on as normally as they could. The strain and the burden of coping under wartime conditions fell on the parents, in particular the mothers, and in some cases the grandparents who threw as good a safety net as possible over their offspring.

Who do you think you are kidding, Mr Hitler? 1939-1940

The outbreak of war on 3rd September 1939 did not catch the country by surprise. War preparations had been underway for more than a year before although clearly at the time of the Munich Agreement in 1938 there was hope that the German dictator could be appeased by agreeing to his demands for the cession of the Sudetenland. Any hope of that disappeared with the German invasion of Poland on 1st September 1939 which then led to the declaration of war between Great Britain and Germany two days later.

A key priority was to ensure that the Government had the necessary powers to put the country onto a war footing in readiness for the outbreak and to maintain that for the duration. The advent of war signalled a significant shift in the role that Government played in the everyday life of citizens and for the duration Government actions became increasingly more intrusive. The Emergency Powers (Defence) Act was passed on 24th August 1939 and provided the umbrella for a range of subsequent Defence Regulations and Orders covering the security of the state, public safety and order, ships and aircraft, and the preservation of essential supplies and work. A second Emergency Powers (Defence) Act was passed on 22nd May 1940 and in effect turned the country into a military camp by allowing the Government to issue whatever orders and regulations it deemed necessary without recourse to Parliament. An early Order, issued on 1st September 1939, dealt with restrictions on lighting and brought into force the blackout requirements that became such a feature of everyday life for civilians and military over the following six years.

Several critical defence services were activated or re-activated in the preparations for war. A key part of the defences against aerial attack was the ring of coastal early warning radar stations, code named Chain Home (CH), built by the Royal Air Force to detect and track enemy aircraft. Chain Home was the first early warning radar network in the world, and the first military radar system to reach operational status. By 1937 five stations, covering the approaches to London, were installed and began full-time operation in 1938. The first operational tests that year, using early units, demonstrated the difficulties in relaying useful information to the fighter pilots. This led to the formation of the first integrated ground-controlled interception network, called the Dowding system, which collected and filtered this information into a single view of the airspace and was subsequently to be a crucial factor in winning the Battle of

Britain. Dozens of CH stations covering the majority of the eastern and southern coasts of the UK, along with a complete ground network with thousands of miles of private telephone lines, were ready by the time the war began in 1939. RAF Truleigh Hill was one of these radar stations, established by 4th June 1940.

The CH network proved decisive during the Battle of Britain in 1940; it could detect enemy aircraft while they were still forming up over France, giving RAF commanders ample time to marshal their fighter planes directly in the path of the raid. This had the effect of multiplying the effectiveness of the RAF to the point that it was as if they had three times as many fighters, allowing them to defeat the larger German force but not, however, without incurring significant losses.

The Observer Corps had been formed in the 1920s initially as a Raid Reporting System responsible for the visual detection, identification, tracking and reporting of aircraft over Great Britain, and eventually becoming known as the Observer Corps. At the end of September 1938 the Observer Corps was mobilized for one week and this highlighted a number of organizational and technical shortcomings which allowed for the development of solutions to resolve these. A series of exercises held throughout 1939 fine-tuned the command and control functions and these continued to evolve throughout the war. During the Battle of Britain and subsequently the Chain Home radar defence system was able to warn of enemy aircraft approaching the British coast, but once having crossed the coastline the Observer Corps provided the only means of tracking their position and passing this vital information to Fighter Command. In April 1941 the Observer Corps was granted the title *Royal* by King George VI as a result of their key role during the Battle of Britain; the Royal Observer Corps then became a uniformed civil defence organization administered by RAF Fighter Command. The ROC was manned by volunteers from every walk of life who showed considerable enthusiasm, dedication and professionalism.

Frederick Farren (Bob Farren's father) was one of these while at the same time continuing to run his garage in Cowfold. Before the war he served as a sergeant in the West Sussex Special Constabulary but then transferred to the Observer Corps at the end of August 1939; he operated from the Sussex HQ which was stationed at the Drill Hall, Denne Road, Horsham, from where the movements of all aircraft across Sussex were plotted, and information passed on to Fighter Command.

The Air Raid Warden's Service had been established in 1937 and training in Air Raid Precautions became available during 1938 and in the months leading to the outbreak of war. Between the 8th and 9th July 1939, the West Sussex ARP services participated in a Regional exercise between 10 pm and 4 am on those nights. The notice issued by the Clerk of the County Council dated the 28th June stated:

"The darkening of areas exposed to air attack may be expected to be an essential feature of the defence of this country in time of war, and useful information on the best means of effecting this may be derived from the present exercise.

Householders and all other occupiers of premises are accordingly asked to assist by ensuring that lights in their premises are extinguished or screened by dark curtains or blinds between 10pm and 4 o'clock in the early morning of the 9th July. It is particularly desirable that external lights and other lights directly visible from the sky should be extinguished or screened. As lighting in streets will be restricted, vehicles should, so far as possible, keep off the roads during the darkened period. Where vehicular traffic must move through the darkened areas, drivers are asked to proceed with their side and rear lamps only, but they can use their headlights at any time when this seems desirable on the grounds of safety.

Air raid warning signals will be sounded at 10pm. From 11 pm until 1am the ARP Services in the County will be actively engaged. Harmless explosions and flares will be used to indicate places where bombs are dropped.

It is hoped that the public will not impede the ARP services by crowding at the sites of incidents."

This of course was the precursor of the blackout restrictions that were to be endured for the next six years.

ARP wardens were appointed for each city, town and village. They were responsible for ensuring the blackout was observed, they sounded air raid sirens, safely guided people into public air raid shelters, issued and checked gas masks, evacuated areas around unexploded bombs, rescued people where possible from bomb damaged properties, located temporary accommodation for those who had been bombed out, and reported to their control centre about incidents such as fires, and called in other services as required.

For Cowfold and the surrounding area, seven men served as ARP wardens including: Mr Reginald Quick the school headmaster, who was appointed Deputy Controller; Luigi Papa; Frederick Slocombe (until he was called up in 1940); Tom Mills; and Sid Trenaman. The ARP post was at the Old Reading Room in Station Road which was manned 24 hours a day by volunteers. One of these was Mrs Adelaide Roberts who lived with her husband Frederick at Cowfold Lodge; Bob Farren used to practice his French with her for a couple of hours in the evening.

Cowfold's air raid siren was sited behind George Oliver's bakery on the Bolney road; although demolished now its footings can still be seen. Near the siren and behind Charlie Belton's blacksmith's shop was the fire station manned by an auxiliary fire unit with Charlie Belton as the head of unit. They used a trailer drawn by car on which there was a pump and hoses but the firemen had to find sources of water depending on where the fire was; fire hydrants were sited in Station Road between Bill Ireland's saddlery shop and Elm Grove and in the roadway at Frederick Farren's shop (Sussex House). Alternative water supplies were available from ponds to the north-east of Potter's Cottages and south-east of Thornden stables. There was also a 10,000 gallon static tank opposite the Post Office in Station Road and several wells. Fire extinguishers were positioned at Thornden Stables, Fowlers' workshops and the Church nave, and stirrup pumps were sited at Council Cottages, at St Peter's School, at Fowler's wheelwrights' shop, at the Church Tower and at the ARP post.

The Women's Voluntary Service (WVS) was established in June 1938 to prepare women for civil defence work. By September 1939, the WVS had 336,000 members, increasing to 1 million members during the war. One of the main tasks of the WVS was to recruit women for ARP services. They also ran field kitchens and rest centres for people made homeless by bombing; provided canteens at railway stations for soldiers and sailors; escorted children being evacuated; ran clothing centres for those who had lost all their possessions; operated car pools once petrol rationing was introduced; helped people salvage their personal belongings from bombed-out houses; and undertook domestic work in hospitals and clinics. The WVS was also the official "sock darner" for the Army - darning 38,000 pairs a week for British and American soldiers! Among those who joined the WVS from Cowfold was Miss Hilda Underhill, Governess at Capon's Farm, Miss Nellie Hermon living at Clock House, Miss Dot Hills a shorthand typist living at "The Gables" on the Bolney Road and Mrs May Trott a widow living at "Bunton" on the Henfield Road.

* * *

In the preparations for war, there was a real concern that the Germans would use gas attacks on civilians; only twenty years earlier the use of gas and gas masks had featured significantly in the fighting on the Western Front during WW1. So by September 1939 around 38 million gas masks had been issued to families, including babies, along with specific instructions about their use and practice drills to ensure people knew how to use them. This included practice for school children at school. Mary Matthews recalls: *"I do remember having the mask in Standard 1 and 2 which was Mr Slocombe's class. We used to have to go to school with the gas mask in a cardboard box slung over our shoulder with string. I also remember at the beginning of the war, a lorry coming to the school once which was used for gas mask practice; we had to put on our gas masks and they filled the lorry with tear gas and we had to go in- so many at a time. I can remember going into the back of the lorry with my gas mask on and it steaming up; we were only in there for a few minutes but I remember coming out panting and taking the gas mask off."* Barbara Ross remembers Miss Archard having to do gas mask checks at school. This involved the children putting on their masks and Miss Archard holding what looked like a floor polish tin to the bottom of the mask; the child had to breathe in and if the tin was sucked onto the end of the mask it was working. However the visors steamed up quickly. Barbara also recalls that her brother John who was a baby at the time had a big enough gas mask to lay him in.

Gas masks in their small cardboard boxes and string to sling over the shoulder became a regular sight in the street and home; in the event they were never needed. However the boxes were not very durable so it was not long before some people replaced theirs with cases made out of leatherette material with a fastening stud.

The 1939 Register (see Appendix A) records Beatrice Dickins as a "gas officer" as well as a Voluntary Aid Detachment (VAD) nurse.

Home defence on land had been the responsibility of the Territorial Army and the Royal Defence Corps since the end of WW1; the latter consisted of regular army soldiers who were either too old or unfit for front line duties. As Germany under the Nazis began to rearm in the 1930s, there was political pressure in Britain to modernise and re-equip the Armed Forces. As a result the Royal Defence Corps was disbanded and National Defence Companies were established in 1936 as part of the Territorial Army, on a county or city basis. They were responsible for protecting vulnerable points in the country and initially were open to ex-members of the Forces and normally for men aged between 45 and 60 years. As war appeared more inevitable, some of these requirements were changed. On 9th May 1939, Lieutenant Colonel Charles Godman, President of the Cowfold District branch of the British Legion issued a special circular asking for men between 45 to 51 years to join "*to serve the localities from which they are recruited, if possible*". Companies were made up of platoons comprising a subaltern, a sergeant, two corporals, two lance-corporals and thirty men. Their duties included patrolling vulnerable places on eight hour shifts. Enlistment was for 4 years and re-engagement for 1, 2, 3 or 4 years for which the men received a gratuity of £5 as well as pay and allowances in line with similar ranks in the Territorial Army. For Sussex, the aim was to recruit 350 men.

The National Defence Companies were mobilised on 25th and 26th August 1939, a week before war was declared. In November 1939, the Companies were formed into battalions attached to regular army regiments and renamed Home Service Battalions. They guarded vulnerable points and prisoner of war camps in the United Kingdom throughout the rest of the war.

* * *

Another real concern was the threat of aerial bombardment of the civilian population who lived in key towns and cities. The world had already witnessed the devastation of a town and the killing of civilians inflicted by aerial bombardment in the German bombing of the Spanish town of Guernica in April 1937 during the Spanish Civil war; an estimated 300 civilians died during the attack which lasted around two hours. So preparations for the mass movement of civilians away from areas at high risk from air raids started with a committee chaired by Sir John Anderson who was asked to recommend how this could be done. That committee reported to Parliament in July 1938 and recommended that:

- Evacuation should not be compulsory;
- Production in large industrial towns should continue but non-essential personnel could be evacuated;
- Accommodation for evacuees should be provided in private homes under powers of compulsory billeting;
- The initial costs of evacuation would be borne by the Government but those who could afford to should contribute; and
- To meet the need for parents who could not afford to evacuate their children, school groups in the charge of their teachers should be sent to reception areas.

As the situation in Europe deteriorated further towards war, so preparations for evacuation accelerated. Official estimates put the population of Great Britain in the summer of 1939 at 45 million of which around 13 million were living in areas that would need to be evacuated. It was also estimated that around 18 million people were living in areas that were deemed reception areas for evacuees. The Ministry of Health defined four main categories of evacuee:

- Pregnant women;
- Mothers with children under 5 years of age;
- School children aged between 5 and 14; and

- Blind and handicapped children where evacuation was feasible.

Significant work was done to prepare the reception areas for receiving evacuees. In the weeks before war was declared, 100,000 visitors investigated over 5 million homes throughout the country for suitability to take evacuees, assessing surplus accommodation on the basis of one person per habitable room including kitchens and bathrooms. Value judgements were also made on individual situations such as the age of the householders (the elderly or infirm were exempted from taking evacuees), or whether the householder would be out of the house all day so unable to provide for school age children. These assessments were made purely on a numerical basis; no attempt was made (and maybe could not have been made) to profile evacuees or match background and character to potential hosts.

By the end of August 1939, preparations had been completed and the order to commence evacuation was given at 11.07 am on 31st August. The next day Operation Pied Piper was launched and over the next four days nearly one and a half million evacuees left the cities that were likely to be the targets for German bombing- the largest single movement of civilians in the history of the country. The authorities celebrated this mass movement as a success, and numerically it was. But for the evacuees and for their host families it was an immense shock, as it was for mothers and fathers who had to say goodbye to their children not knowing when or if they would ever see them again. There were distressing scenes at railway stations as mothers faced the heart-breaking wrench of having to see their children leave clutching gas masks, small suitcases and provisions for the journey, and wearing luggage labels. And when they arrived at their destination the evacuees were squeezed into village halls, marquees, churches and schools to wait to be selected by host families. For many evacuees the experience was similar to a cattle or slave market. This also often led to family members being separated or mixed and matched. Some were selected quickly; others were not immediately selected and it was left to the billeting officers to knock on doors well into the night in the first few days desperately trying to house the unfortunate left-behinds.

In many cases there was a significant clash of cultures; country folk viewed many of the evacuee children as verminous, badly dressed and ill-mannered whereas evacuees reacted strongly against outside earthen lavatories, oil lamps and cold water taps. That said, for many evacuee children the experience was positively life changing and many became very fond of their foster parent or parents and of the surroundings they had moved to. But others found it difficult to adjust to country life and soon returned to the city.

Cowfold was one of the reception areas and received two waves of evacuees in the first few days; the billeting officers were Mary Hanley and Olive Fowler. On 2nd September 175 mothers and children arrived followed two days later by 97 children and 9 teachers from Christchurch Parish School, Croydon. Among the Croydon School teachers were Miss Ada Browning who was billeted with Jack and Gladys Faires at "Fairhill" on the Henfield Road, and Miss Joan Cordell who was billeted with the Reverend William Sandberg and his wife Ethel at the Vicarage. In addition 27 children came from St Andrew's, Streatham, 2 from St Matthew's Brixton, 5 from St Leonard's Brixham and 6 from Heathfield Road School, Streatham. Jean Parsons remembers seeing the evacuees arriving at Cowfold by coach, carrying cases and looking very sad.

The 1939 Register, taken on 29th September records 76 evacuees' names only because others' names have been redacted so those individuals cannot be placed. But Eileen Benson, third daughter of Charlie and Gertrude Benson, who at the beginning of the war was working for the Lovett-Camerons at Brook Hill House as a kitchen maid, remembers 25 evacuees being taken in, including Joan Harris and Joan Huggett:

"Everything was removed from the drawing room which was a very large room, then 25 new mattresses were laid on the floor where they were to sleep. Along one side of the room they made up shelves for the children to put their own belongings, although they hadn't much with them anyway. This of course made a lot of extra work, especially in the kitchen. This was particularly so after food rationing was introduced in January 1940 when items such as butter, bacon and sugar were limited to a few ounces a week each; it took a lot of working out with Cook and myself to make it all go around, but it gave me a lot of experience towards becoming a cook."

Mary Matthews remembers Alan and Vera Cheal who lodged at Vachers, Kent Street, Colin Rudling remembers Phyllis Campbell who lodged with his family at Woodside Close, Shermanbury, Pat Ferri remembers Mrs Marie Ashman and her two year old daughter Frances who lodged with Sid and Ethel Trenaman at Cottlands on the Horsham Road and Maureen and Irene Collier who lodged with the Misses Hoper at Hill House Farm, and Jean and Barbara Ross remember Silvia Wilcox who lodged with Ernie and Margaret Reed at Brook Farm Cottages. Bob Farren remembered a mother and small boy, probably aged one, being billeted at Sussex House: *"I think they came from Streatham but they didn't stay long. The mother couldn't stand it because there weren't the range of shops she was used to and she kept complaining that there was nothing to do."*

Adapting to village and country life was difficult for some of the evacuee children. Colin Rudling remembers that:

"They made quite an impact in the school; they were definitely different to us and we were a bit in awe of them at first. They

were louder, more full of themselves. But then we discovered that they were afraid of cows and the woods in the dark because they had never seen cows or been in the woods at night; it terrified them whereas we had just grown up with all that. So somehow this restored the balance and after that we got on quite well with most of them." Pat Ferri also recalls that: *"There was one boy who was a talented artist who lodged with the Cannels at Singers. I remember bringing him home because he was scared of the walk from the village in the pitch black. I didn't mind because I had grown up with it but he hadn't experienced that before."*

That influx of children including the whole school from Croydon meant that St Peter's School was not able to accommodate the pupils. As was the case in other parts of the county and country, a double shift system was put in place with local children being taught at the school in the morning and evacuees in the afternoon. Slightly later the Village Hall was used to teach evacuee children so relieving some of the pressure on the school. There was also discussion about re-opening the school at Shermanbury but it was subsequently decided not to do this.

* * *

An overriding concern for officials involved in planning for war was the supply of food. As an island Britain had some advantages in terms of the Channel being a defensive barrier to any invader, but as an island it was also vulnerable to attack on its supply routes to and from the countries of the Empire and the west. This weakness had been ruthlessly exposed and exploited during WW1 when German U boats wreaked havoc to shipping and therefore to Britain's supply lines. Rationing had been introduced to eke out the food and other supplies that were available but in addition there had been a strong drive to encourage increased food production from the land matched by the enthusiastic formation of the Women's Land Army in 1915, increased voluntary work and even the enlistment of school children to help with harvesting the food that was home grown. The same issues and similar responses were now to become a key part of the struggle for survival during WW2.

In 1939 two thirds of British food needs were met by imports (20 million tons a year) including 88% of the nation's consumption of wheat, about 70% of its cheese and sugar, nearly 80% of fruits and about 70% of cereals and fats. Britain also imported more than half of its meat, and relied on imported feed to support its domestic meat production. Farming had been in recession since the end of WW1 because of cheaper imports and agricultural wages were correspondingly depressed; in 1938 agricultural prices were only a third above pre WW1 prices and there was hardly any incentive to farm efficiently. Farmers had also concentrated their efforts largely on livestock- cattle, pigs and sheep- at the expense of growing crops. Now with the impending war with Germany that trend had to be reversed and the plough had to become a weapon of war. Mary Matthews recalls that: *"At the farm we had to grow corn. I remember the fields being ploughed up and corn being sown and being harvested later"*.

Farming still relied heavily on the horse and mechanization was not widespread; in 1939 there were 20 horses to each tractor. Mark Matthews, farming at Wilcox Farm along Kent Street, never possessed a tractor until 1952; all the farming was done by hand or by using horses and carts.

Milk was an important part of the diet particularly for children but was centrally controlled by the Milk Marketing Board (MMB). At Wilcox farm, Mary's mother was stopped from making butter because the bulk of their milk had to go to the MMB, collected at the gate in big churns by lorry, leaving only enough for the family's own needs.

War Agricultural Committees (War Ags) had been established in 1915 with the aim of increasing agricultural production and better managing the country's limited agricultural resources. They were re-formed from 2nd September 1939 under the Cultivation of Lands Order of that year with the immediate task of bringing into production another one and a half million acres of land; they were given wide powers over the cultivation and management of land, over ending tenancies for poorly run farms and over taking possession of land. To establish whether farms were being managed efficiently and could be made more efficient, each farm was surveyed over the two years from the outbreak of war and its production measured by annual returns. Farmers' competence was graded by A, B and C classifications, C being a condemnation of the farmer which could lead to him being thrown off the farm and it being taken into the possession of the War Ag.

A Ministry of Food was established on 8th September 1939 as an additional player in the drive to enable Britain to feed itself, alongside the existing Ministry of Agriculture and Fisheries; its role was to oversee and control all food sold in the country and to increase nutrition for everyone. A key factor in maintaining nutrition was the availability of milk in particular for children. So too was the replacement for vitamins which had been provided by imported fruit which was now found in locally available fruits such as blackcurrants and rosehips.

Although farming was a reserved occupation during the war, additional labour resources were needed if the demands of increased production were to be met. So the Women's Land Army (WLA) which had been established during the First World War was re-mobilized in June 1939 under the leadership of Lady Gertrude Denman but under the control of the Ministry of Agriculture and Fisheries. By the end of

1939 4,500 women had joined the WLA (rising to 80,300 four years later). Regional representatives oversaw the placing and care of the girls who in 1940 were paid 28 shillings a week for those aged 18 and over and 22/6d for those under 18; from that wage board and lodging was deducted at 14 shillings and 12/6d respectively. Land Army girls worked on the farms in the Cowfold and surrounding areas during the war including, as Mary Matthews remembers, a girl called Pearl who worked for Joseph Johnson at Cooper's Farm and who eventually married him after his wife Hilda had died early on in the war. And a May Jones worked as a dairy maid at South Lodge towards the end of the war. Jean and Barbara Ross joined the Girl Guides in Henfield during the war and remember both the Captain and the Lieutenant being in the WLA and working on the nearby market gardens; their Aunt Joan was also a member of the WLA.

* * *

The announcement of war with Germany on 3ʳᵈ September 1939 was one of those days when just about everyone remembered where they were and what they were doing; just as they remembered D-Day on 6ᵗʰ June 1944 or VE Day on 8ᵗʰ May 1945. Unlike the announcement of war with Germany in 1914, there was no outpouring of patriotism and volunteer enlistment this time. Memories of what was supposed to have been "the war to end all wars" only twenty years earlier were still too fresh. The reaction of Cowfold villagers to Chamberlain's announcement on that September Sunday morning was one of either despair or resignation. There was also a strong feeling among some villagers, particularly the women that despite the war they would need to try to carry on life as normally as possible.

Gordon Buxton had had a tough time during WW1, including having to carry the body of his commanding officer Lieutenant

Colonel Hermon from the field during the battle of Arras in April 1917 and writing to tell the Colonel's widow. Jessica Buxton recalls: *"The worst thing I remember when war broke out was hearing Chamberlain making the announcement. I remember my father putting his head on the table and crying because he knew what war was".*

Bob Farren remembers:

"Chamberlain's announcement on 3rd September 1939 was half expected although there's no doubt that the generation that had survived the First World War was very apprehensive. I remember I was sitting in Sussex House on a sofa in the sitting room which backed onto a window which looked out onto the churchyard. My father had the radio on and we heard Mr Chamberlain's speech and I remember my father saying "Well we know what we've got to do and this one won't be over by Christmas". I think that was a common attitude amongst the older generation".

Pat Ferri had a white pigeon as a pet which came down one day and sat on her grandparents' coal-house roof and never went away. He became very tame and thought he was a hen; he would walk into the hen house after the hens at night and perch on a roost with them and come out with them in the morning.

"I remember Chamberlain's announcement on 3rd September 1939. My grandparents had the wireless on. My grandparents took it very seriously because they had been through WW1 and had lost a son; another son who survived the war nevertheless developed a sort of twitch- a tic- which they said was due to shell shock. So they were very sombre at hearing the news and it was only 20 years since the end of what was supposed to be "the war to end all wars". I was scared stiff of the news. I could read early and

I read about and saw the photographs of the Spanish Civil War in 1936. I didn't of course know about the privations and horrors of war but nevertheless I could see that this was a nasty event. So when war was announced I went and picked up my pigeon which I called "Pidge" and cried and told him".

Not everyone was at home when war was declared. Mary Matthews:

"I can remember Sunday 3rd September 1939 quite plainly because my sister and I were staying with my grandmother at a place called Milland on the border with Hampshire. My mum came straight over to pick us up and bring us home. She said "Now that war is declared you have to stay at home- no going over to grandmother's house anymore".

And Elizabeth Chase had been visiting her father's sister- Auntie Gertie- in Horsham at the time.

At St Peter's school the children had not yet returned from their summer holidays. The school log book, written by Mr Quick, refers to the outbreak of war somewhat laconically- and this would be a feature of much of the reporting in the log book during the war; perhaps this was just Mr Quick's style or it may also have been part of a concerted effort to carry on life as normally as possible. The log merely says:

"During the holiday war has been declared against Germany. Teachers reassembled for duties on 28th August preparing for the evacuation of London children in Cowfold and other areas, the headmaster Mr R.H.P Quick acting as liaison officer for Horsham Southern Rural District comprising Cowfold, Jolesfield, Lower Beeding, Nuthurst, Shipley, Coolham, Billingshurst, Southwater and Itchingfield".

In 1939 there were 80,000 civilian German or Austrian nationals living in Britain as well as many Italians. 600 were immediately interned at the outbreak of war and another 9,000 were restricted in where they went and with whom they associated. In May 1940 after the fall of France and with the threat of German invasion, all aliens who had not taken out naturalisation papers were interred; most of them were released starting in early 1941 once the threat of invasion had receded. It is not known whether the Papa family living in Cowfold were affected but given that Luigi Papa served as an ARP warden it is likely that he and his family were not regarded as posing any sort of risk.

* * *

The expectation was that the Germans would start bombing as soon as war was declared and indeed air raid sirens were sounded almost immediately after Chamberlain had stopped speaking. Elizabeth Chase, who had been visiting her aunt in Horsham, recalls: *"A siren went off as we were going down the road to the Carfax. We had to turn back as she* [Elizabeth's aunt] *had a metallic Anderson shelter in the garden. People were told to take cover but it was a false alarm"*.

No attack came and this was the start of the so-called "Phoney War" which lasted from 3rd September 1939 to 10th May 1940. During this period there was only one limited land offensive on the Western Front when French troops invaded Germany's Saar region with the intention of helping Poland which the Germans had invaded on 1st September 1939, but this achieved very little. There were plans developed to damage the German war effort, including an attempt to stop the Germans accessing Norway's iron ore deposits, but again these proved to be either ineffectual or too little too late. The Germans launched attacks at sea in the autumn and winter against British aircraft carriers and destroyers, sinking several, and from October 1939 launched air raids on British ships. And in April 1940 the Germans invaded Norway and Denmark forcing British troops to be evacuated in June. But at home civilians began to wonder what all the fuss was about and fears of immediate attack dissipated. Mothers and children who had been evacuated from cities and towns now began to drift back despite appeals from the Government to stay put. By January 1940 over one third of evacuee mothers and children had returned home - 350,000 children during the autumn of 1939- leaving around 570,000 evacuees in the reception areas.

However the threat to British food supplies remained a constant from the start of the war and strangling those supplies was a key plank of the total German offensive against Britain. In 1939 and subsequently Germany relied heavily on attacks on shipping by U-boats and pocket battleships to try to starve Britain into submission- what came to be called the "Battle of the Atlantic". Later those attacks would in addition focus on preventing supplies of armaments, equipment and personnel coming across the Atlantic from the United States and Canada and would complement the loss of raw materials such as rubber from parts of the Empire following the entry of Japan to the war. In 1939 800 tons of fruit and vegetables were destroyed at sea rising to 22,000 tons in 1940. These and other losses and the ongoing attacks on shipping led to two main consequences for the British population.

First was the imposition of rationing. From 23rd September 1939 petrol was rationed to seven gallons a month allowing for journeys of no more than 200 miles although certain professions such as doctors, the emergency services and farmers were given larger allowances. The civilian petrol allowance was withdrawn altogether on 1st July 1942 and then was available only to official users such as the emergency services; petrol for authorised users was dyed and it was an offence to use this for non-essential purposes.

Apart from being rationed the sale of petrol was also confined to a small number of filling stations- the nearest to Cowfold was at Buck Barn. Bob Farren remembers that his father's garage and the Bridge Garage on the Henfield Road were not allowed to sell petrol at all during the war and for a time the army took over the pumps.

Petrol rationing was followed on 8th January 1940 by rationing of bacon, butter and sugar and then other food stuffs, including milk. Allowances fluctuated throughout the war, but on average one adult's weekly ration was 4 ozs (113 g) of bacon and ham (about four thin slices), one shilling and ten pence worth of meat (about 227g of minced beef), 2 ozs (57 g) of butter, 8 ozs (227 g) of sugar, 2 ozs (57 g) of tea, 2 ozs (57g) of cheese, 3 pints of milk, 113g of margarine, and 113g of cooking fat. Other foods such as canned meat, fish, rice, condensed milk, breakfast cereals, biscuits and vegetables were available but in limited quantities on a points system.

Shell eggs were rationed from June 1941 to one egg per adult per week. Fresh vegetables, fruit, bread and fish were not rationed but prices increased and the commodities became harder to obtain; some fruit such as bananas and lemons disappeared from the shops altogether. Those living in the countryside were in many respects better off than city or town dwellers since there were greater opportunities for foraging and for obtaining wild meat such as rabbits or pigeons to supplement the diet. None of the interviewees for this book remember being hungry during the war. Here is Barbara Ross:

"I don't know how she managed it but Mum could make a meal out of nothing. She was great. We were lucky in a way being in the country rather than in a town because there was always food around- home grown vegetables, chickens, pigs and rabbits. So we never went hungry. I remember Mum preserving eggs in isingglass

in a great big crock; but I don't remember how she preserved them. I also remember salted runner beans; you just packed runner beans with coarse salt which took the water out of the beans and preserved them. They all go grey and of course when you came to eat them, you had to soak and soak them to get rid of the salt. I can also remember her bottling fruit in Kilner jars.

I can remember being around at Mrs Weller's one afternoon– Mr Weller was a handyman at Longhouse and they lived in a cottage near us; she was enormous so she never got out so we used to pop round to see her because she was a jolly sort of person– and I felt hungry so went home, raided the cake tin for a piece of madeira cake and ate it. Mum comes round later and asks "Where's the cake gone?" It was supposed to have shared between the three of us but I had eaten it".

Her elder sister Jean also remembers picking blackberries, wild strawberries and mushrooms on their way home from school to supplement the diet.

Improvisation was an essential part of coping with rationing restrictions and housewives soon became adept at finding ways to eke out what was available and turning an old or worn out item into something more useful. Jean and Barbara Ross' mother Mary was particularly skilful at making do and mending. Barbara remembers a second hand coat of hers, that was a very faded Harris Tweed but whose inside lining of mauve and purple fleck was still quite fresh, which her mother unpicked, turned inside out and put back together. Her sewing machine was in constant use including making cycling capes out of a ground sheet for the girls when they were at High School.

Barbara also remembers a man who lived up the lane from Longhouse and who kept a few Jersey cows, putting the milk into shallow trays to skim off the cream. The girls would collect some of this skimmed milk, carefully take off the top surface again, take it home and put it in a Kilner jar and then shake it to make a pat of butter.

Rationing carried with it requirements that left a lasting mark on those who had to endure it. The ration card and coupons, including for sweets, and clothing coupons which were introduced later, became an essential feature of life in the same way as having to carry at all times the National Identity card, the cardboard box containing the gas mask, and queuing. For most rationed items each person had to register at chosen shops which were provided with enough food for rationed customers, and which could only provide that food in exchange for the relevant coupons. Pat Ferri remembers:

"The [ration] books had to be renewed regularly and very often the eldest child- and I was the only child in the household- was sent because it took nearly all day to renew. There were well meaning women who used to do this arduous task in the village- I can't remember whether it was at the school or the village hall. You also had to register with a particular supplier for certain goods- the butcher, Mr Goacher in our case, Sprinks for our groceries. One part of the ration book was devoted to points and they could be spent anywhere- such as sweets and tinned goods. There were two emergency points in the village; one a big brick built garage type building on the north side of the Red Lion and one at the Monastery. Stocks of food were held there and I suppose these would have been used if we had been cut off in some way. Distribution would have been done by the WVS which was a well-oiled organisation".

Barbara Ross has similar memories:

"Ration books were issued by the Ministry of Food so we had to go to Horsham where the Ministry had offices to get them. They also issued emergency ration coupons which we had to get when we went to stay with our grandmother for her to be able to get our rations while we stayed at her place.

Once you had got your ration book you had to register with a particular butcher for meat, a particular grocer for those things- we always went to Sprinks'. But sweets and clothing coupons you could use anywhere that sold them.

The ration book as a whole lasted for about three months because there were different pages for different things. Mum gave us our sweet coupons and once they had been used that was it until the next batch. So every quarter we would have to go back to Horsham to get a new ration book.

Pretty much everything was rationed, in particular food, although you could occasionally get a rabbit from a local farmer. We had dried milk and dried eggs which were provided by the Ministry of Food in big blue and silver tins. It may have been that we were issued with those because we were children. We also used to get cod liver oil and concentrated orange. Film for a camera was hard to get hold of. Timothy White's in Horsham used to sell one film per customer and we used that mainly for pictures of us and John to send to Dad".

The strict rationing regulations inevitably meant that there would be people who looked for and took opportunities to circumvent the rules or even to indulge in "black marketing". The black market was a direct commercial response to shortages of food and other supplies and was rife in the countryside as secluded rural spots proved ideal places from which to operate. Cigarettes and alcohol were never rationed but were in short supply so were a natural target for the black marketer despite the hefty penalties if caught which could mean a fine of £500 or two years in prison; and on top of the fine offenders were required to pay three times the value of the items they had been caught selling. Petrol was another prime target for the black market. There is no hard evidence of black marketing in Cowfold but it would not have been surprising if the butcher or grocer had not had some items available "under the counter". One instance of rule flouting in Cowfold in 1940 was reported in the local newspaper:

"A butcher who was stated to have supplied to an unregistered customer a joint of beef which he labelled "pork" because that was an unrationed commodity, was fined £10 and costs of £1 12s by the Magistrates at Horsham. Defendant Arthur Lyne Dixon, butcher of Palmeston House, Cowfold, pleaded guilty to the offence that, being a registered retailer, he supplied a customer, the holder of a general ration book for household consumption, with a rationed food he not then being the retailer with whom the customer was registered in accordance with the directions of the Ministry of Food. The case was one of a number brought by the Horsham Rural District Food Control Committee".

The unregistered customer, a Mrs Helen Wadey of 30 Stable Cottages, Lower Beeding was fined £2 and given a month in which to pay.

But food shortages also meant that the community tended to pull together more strongly. Elizabeth Chase, living with her mother and grandparents at "Chalfield", Shermanbury, remembers:

"People were more benevolent with each other. Everybody knew everybody and if you had some apples left over from your apple tree, you would share them. There was a much stronger sense of community and reliance on each other. I think that was because of the war because everyone was in the same boat and in peril. It

wasn't as though you were poking your nose in; it was a genuine desire to help and get us through this awful situation".

The second main consequence of food shortages was that people were urged and many became, as self-sufficient as possible. The First World War had seen a need for the country to increase its ability to grow and produce as much food as possible itself so the threat faced by Britain in WW2 was not an unexpected or new experience. But this time round the drive for self-sufficiency was significantly stronger.

The National Allotments Society had been founded in 1901 to encourage people to take up allotments, to grow their own produce and to make better use of spare land, including railway edges, ornamental gardens and lawns. By 1939 there were 815,000 allotments across the country and by 1943 that number had increased to 1.4 million. The Produce Guild had been established in 1938 to encourage people to grow more of their own food and by the end of that year there were 48 county branches. Surplus produce was sold via Women's Institute registered market stalls of which there were 30 by the end of 1939. But by far the most memorable initiative to increase home food production and boost morale was the *"Dig for Victory"* leafleting and information campaign which had its origins in the early months of the war but really took off from the autumn of 1940, although it did not find favour with everyone; a number of exhortatory posters appeared including probably the best known- a photographic image of a magnified left boot on a spade which was issued in 1940. The campaign was complemented by Ministry of Agriculture bulletins, by radio programmes and by the available gardening magazines such as *"The Smallholder"* and *"Amateur Gardening"* all of which gave advice on better growing techniques, supplemented by the available expertise of the Royal Horticultural Society.

Most houses in Cowfold and the surrounding area had room for chickens and rabbits and perhaps a pig or two; Bob Farren remembers that people who had chickens were given an extra allocation of grain. He also recalls that *"depending on how much garden was available, people could grow their own vegetables. We didn't have much of a garden at Sussex House but there was an elderly man, a Mr Freeman* [probably Mr Walter Freeman who lived with his wife Rose at 2 Margaret Cottages] *who kept Mother supplied with vegetables. Across the road my grandparents had a bit of garden where they could grow vegetables"*. Barbara Ross also recalls that: *"Dad had a vegetable plot and Mr Weller had one as well. When Dad wasn't there it was too much for Mum to do and old Albert, who was a semi tramp or vagrant who lived in a brick built dog kennel at Oakendene, came up over the course of a few days and dug the garden and Mum just fed him- that was all he wanted. He'd had to walk up from the village and then do the digging and he wasn't young"*.

Barbara also remembers having a pet black and white rabbit called Blackie: *"We had a lovely meal that Mum said was chicken. I later found out that we had eaten Blackie. But Mum had kept the skin, cured it by rubbing in alum and salt petre and then made me a pair of fur mittens. Nothing was wasted"*.

During 1940 there was a proliferation of "pig clubs" which were usually run as a form of cooperative where a group of local people looked after a number of pigs, collecting swill from the surrounding houses for feed and receiving a part of the pig in return once it was slaughtered, the major part going to the Government and entering the food supply chain. Belonging to a pig club allowed its members a ration of precious imported meal. It is not known for sure whether there were pig clubs operating in and around Cowfold but it is highly likely that that was the case.

For those villagers who didn't have a garden and who wanted to grow their own either because they were encouraged by the Dig for Victory campaign or because they just wanted to supplement their diet, allotments were available just to the south of St Peter's School near the rifle range which was also used by the Cowfold

Home Guard, and also next to the sewage works in Eastlands Lane. The school also "grew its own". The boys had gardening classes one day a week and grew various vegetables including potatoes.

Enthusiasm for the Dig for Victory campaign was dented by the winter of 1939/40. January 1940 was the coldest month on record for almost 50 years and would ultimately become the second coldest January of the 20th century. By the middle of January the Thames had frozen over for the first time in 60 years while Wales on one day suffered a temperature low of -23C. In southern Britain rain fell instead of snow, encasing trees, telegraph and power lines in ice, causing them to collapse. But then it snowed.

At St Peter's School, Mr Quick recorded that on 22nd December 1939:

"The water supply failed at Oakendean crossroads owing to the intense cold".

On 11th January 1940:

"Owing to the very severe weather (26 degrees of frost) one of the pedestals in the girls' WCs has burst".

On 21st January:

"During the week extra fires have had to be lit owing to the intense cold and in order to save heating apparatus".

On 29th January:

"During the week-end there has been a decided drop in temperature. The roads are in such a glassy state owing to the rain falling and freezing on the surface so that there is nearly an inch

of frozen surface. Only 18 children [out of a total school of 131] have attended as snow is falling heavily".

On 30th January:

"Snow has been falling all night and there are drifts in the playground varying from 1ft to 3ft deep. There are 35 children present and these are having boots and clothing dried. Three of the school doors have frozen up during the night owing to the drifting snow. Icicles are three feet long on the gutterings".

And then on 2nd February:

"The weather conditions continue so bad that children are now failing badly. There was a drift of snow of 2ft 6 inches whilst at the door the snow had piled up nearly 5ft. This had to be cleared. A sharp thaw set in on Sunday afternoon and the snow is now clearing rapidly. Outside temperature is now 45F against an average of 26F last week".

Amazing! And equally amazing is that the school stayed open- but this was probably more to do with the fact that Mr Quick lived on site and many of the children lived in the village and could walk to school.

But alongside the cold weather and often because of it, there was a lot of illness. On January 8th 1940 the school log records that children had heavy colds and there were several cases of chicken pox. And on 31st January there were many cases of influenza in the area and in neighbouring schools, as well as scarlet fever and measles.

* * *

It is not known exactly how many men from the village and surrounding area were called up at the outbreak of war or subsequently. But among those who did join the Forces were Bert Sayers (Pat Sayers' father) who was called up in 1939, joined the Medical Corps and was posted to North Africa; Eric Vincent's father who was called up in 1940, joined the RAF as a road transport driver and was posted to Burma; Colin Rudling's father who joined the Royal Electrical Mechanical Engineers and served with the 8th Army in Africa and Italy; Frederick Slocombe, Assistant Master at St Peter's School who joined the RAF in October 1940, but was shot down over Germany in 1941 and then spent the rest of the war as a prisoner of war- according to Pat Ferri he became a member of the Caterpillar Club who were airmen who had been saved by a parachute after jumping from a plane; Elizabeth Chase's father who was posted to India in 1942/3 on medical work; and Jean and Barbara Ross's father who was called up in 1940 and joined the Royal Sussex Regiment; he was with the regiment at the siege of Tobruk in 1941. Jean and Barbara's father was also a member of the Territorial Army before the war; they remember being on holiday at Bexhill a fortnight or so before war was declared and their father with a lot of other men filling sandbags with the sand from the beach as part of the war preparations. In addition Bob Farren was called up and joined the RAF in 1944 and after training was posted overseas until the end of the war.

It is very hard for us now to appreciate what it must have been like to say goodbye to a loved one who had been called up, not knowing when or if ever, they would return. How many heart-wrenching scenes there must have been with each side trying to put on a brave face. One such scene was played out when Jean and Barbara Ross and their mother Mary, said goodbye to their father Jock at Horsham Station in October 1940. Barbara recalls:

"It was difficult saying goodbye to my father on Horsham Station particularly for my Mum. She was in tears and I was holding her hand and to distract her I said "Ooh Mum look at the pretty pictures" and when she looked up it was advertisements for corsets all along the top of the station steps! She laughed about that afterwards. It was more upsetting for her than for us because as children we didn't really realise what we were in for and the length of time it would be before we saw him again or if we would see him again.

Our only contact with Dad for four and a half years was by mail- aerograms which had to be photographed and reduced. He wouldn't have been able to write often and anything he wrote was censored with words ruled out by blue lines. The only time that my mother knew where he was, was when she was very pregnant with John and she had had this aerogram from Dad. To get past the censors, he devised a sort of code where he would start a line with, for example T, and the next with O and the next with B until the letters spelt out TOBRUK so she knew that that was where he was. That was in June 1941. After that we didn't hear from him for six weeks and during that time Barbara and I developed whooping cough two days before John was due to be born at home, so the district nurse couldn't come nor could the doctor if there was infection in the house. The baby couldn't be born with us nearby so we had to stay at a local farm for six weeks. So it was amazing what our mother had to go through at that time.

Dad was a quartermaster with his regiment and I remember him telling us that most of the time during the siege of Tobruk, he would spend the night behind enemy lines on raids, scavenging for petrol and other things. Afterwards he had an aversion to sand". Jean adds: "Our brother John was an "embarkation baby" born in June 1941, so my Dad never saw him until he returned. A "village" story was that when my mother took John out in the *pram to the village for the first time she met a woman who asked to see the baby and said "Ooh isn't he lovely! And when did Mr Ross go away?"*

* * *

On 10th May 1940 the "Phoney War" came to an abrupt and bloody end when the German Luftwaffe, tanks and troops unleashed the "Blitzkrieg" a new form of coordinated air and ground forces attack that would sweep through Belgium, Holland and France in less than a month. Events unfolded rapidly. On 11th May Chamberlain resigned and was succeeded by Winston Churchill. British Expeditionary Force (BEF) troops, who had been deployed to France in August/September 1939 manoeuvred with the French to try to halt the German advance but were taken by surprise by the German attack through the Ardennes, which crossed the River Meuse on 14th May, broke through the defences and dashed to the Channel coast intending to encircle the Allied armies fighting there. The BEF retreated to the Channel ports, hampered by waves of civilians flooding and blocking the roads in their desperation to escape the German advance. By 26th May the BEF had been forced back into a small enclave around the town of Dunkirk and their evacuation began, coordinated by Admiral Ramsey and code-named Operation Dynamo. The evacuation ended on 4th June by which time 338,226 troops had been saved; a significant part in that success was played by the "little ships"- 700 privately owned motor boats and other vessels which carried troops off the beaches to larger ships waiting further out to sea. The evacuation was called a "miracle" but in reality much of the success was down to the Germans' failure to maintain their attack on the bridgehead around Dunkirk, the RAF's success in preventing the Luftwaffe from making evacuation impossible, and the Royal Navy's, assisted by the Merchant Navy's, success in lifting so many men from the beaches. But heavy losses had been inflicted on the BEF including the loss of most of its equipment which meant that Britain was now very vulnerable to invasion.

One of those rescued from the Dunkirk beaches was George Relf who before the war had worked for Fowlers in Cowfold. But there were others as indicated by Mr Quick's entry in the school log for 28th June:

> *"The considerable fall in attendance [at school on that day] is due to the great number of children in the Infants Room failing with measles but also many parents on BEF leave after the Dunkirk withdrawal".*

Unfortunately there is no indication of the names or the number of those men.

On 11th June Italy entered the war on the side of the Germans and on 22nd June France surrendered and signed an armistice with Germany. Then on 16th July Hitler ordered preparations for the invasion of Britain, code-named Operation Sea Lion.

At home, on 14th May the British Government had called for volunteers to form Local Defence Volunteer (LDV) units: 250,000 volunteers signed up in the first seven days rising to 1.5 million by July. In Sussex the volunteers were formed into 26 battalions and there were platoons recruited in Cowfold and most if not all of the surrounding towns and villages. Initially there were problems about arming the units and many resorted to raiding museums for weapons or equipping themselves with private weapons such as shotguns; although there is no evidence that the men of Cowfold resorted to raiding a museum many had shotguns. This and confusion over the role that the LDV was supposed to play led to complaints and low morale among the recruits and eventually led to the LDV being renamed the Home Guard, at Churchill's insistence, on 22nd July and being properly armed and trained.

The Cowfold Home Guard was commanded initially by Captain Theophilus Kerr-Jones who lived at "Wythe" on the road up to Brook Hill. He was 62 years old at the outbreak of war and retired from his command in 1943. His place was taken by James Goacher, the butcher, who was promoted to Lieutenant. The Cowfold Home Guard included Reg Thomas, Fred Tuck, Mark Matthews (full time for a short time only), and Walter Parsons (Jean Parsons' father). Reg Thomas, who farmed Crateman's Farm, was the platoon sergeant and Dr Thomas Matthews was the medical officer. The platoon used the rifle range just to the south of St Peter's School and, probably after James Goacher took over command, had their HQ at the Olde House, Mr Goacher's premises on The Street.

The Home Guard's role was to act as a secondary defence force, in case of German invasion. In that event they were to try to slow down the German advance even by a few hours in order to give the regular troops time to regroup. They guarded coastal areas and other important places such as airfields, factories and explosives stores, and manned defensive obstacles such as pill boxes and barriers set across routes the enemy was likely to use. Tank traps and pillboxes were sited at Mock Bridge on the road up from Henfield and makeshift barriers were set up across the road from the Red Lion in Cowfold and just further up, across the road from Peacock's stores.

The Home Guard undertook regular night and daytime exercises and patrols. One exercise is recorded in West Grinstead and Partridge Green History Society's account of WW2 entitled *When the Whistle Blew*; permission has kindly been given to reproduce the account here narrated by one of the Home Guard members and written by Colin Rudling.

"Well after that now with our arms, our equipment was complete and it was only a few Sundays after that Vic Greenwood said to us " Next Sunday we're going to have a somewhat more ambitious exercise, we're going to attack Cowfold." Now Cowfold was the next village along the road to Horsham, about 3 miles away, and the Home Guard at Cowfold was going to defend the village and Partridge Green Home Guard were going to attack and see if they could capture the village. And he said "I shall want the first aid men to be there because there might be casualties, so you must bring your stretcher a few blankets, first aid kit and so on".

Cowfold is a little bit smaller than Partridge Green, with one long more or less straight street and at the bottom there's the Bridge Garage, by the Bridge Garage there's a stream and then the road goes gently uphill for about a quarter of a mile, right to the top of Cowfold. We discovered that the first aid post was on the highest point, at the top of Cowfold and we were stationed down by the Bridge Garage.

It was very interesting, there were bangs and run-ins and fighting and so on, and the old ladies going to church wondered what on earth had come to Cowfold that Sunday morning. We stood around and waited when suddenly there was cry "First aid men there's a casualty" and so we went running with our stretcher. And sure enough there he was, lying on the ground.

I recognised him, it was George. George was the cowman at the next farm to mine and George was sixteen stone. When he saw us he grinned and I looked at him and said "Goodness it would be you wouldn't it". He said "Yes, I'm sure I'm going to enjoy this". I knew what we'd got to do, we'd got to carry him a quarter of a mile right through the middle of Cowfold, uphill all the way. He said "Come on undo the stretcher and I'll jump on" and I said "No, don't you do that, you lay still, you don't know who might be watching. We'll lift you on properly." And so we did. We put him on the stretcher, wrapped him up in blankets and we picked him up and off we went, four of us, one on each corner and the corporal bringing up the rear.

We hadn't got very far before Henry (one of the stretcher bearers) suddenly said "Why are you going so fast, I can't keep up, you're forgetting my bad heart". We slowed down a bit, and of course in those days there was very little traffic and so we walked along in the middle of the road and up this slope towards the first aid post. A little farther again there was cry from Henry "Slower, slower I can't keep up". Well eventually he got so puffed we had to put George down in the middle of the road and the corporal said "Here look, I'll take one corner, you walk behind, just try and look important and keep up." And so off we went.

We reached the top of the hill eventually, a little bit puffed but we got our casualty there. Then we turned up a carriage drive, to a small mansion. [This is likely to have been Brookhill House, the home of Captain and Mrs Lovett-Cameron]. *The lady and gentleman who lived there had placed their house at the disposal of the Home Guard that Sunday morning. So in we went, through a French window onto a most beautiful carpet and there we put George down, stretcher and all, in front of the doctor. The doctor was old Doctor Dickens. He was our doctor and I knew him very well and of course he was an officer. So, we uncovered George and there he was. Now for some reason best known to George he had worn that morning a brilliant scarlet pullover underneath his battledress and when the doctor undid his battledress and began to see what was wrong with him, I thought, as I knew the doctor so well, perhaps a little conversation might be useful. So I said "Is he hurt doctor?" Well he said "Hurt, man, hurt, why look at that pullover". After that, of course I thought in the army you don't have a casual conversation with officers even if you know them very well, so I said nothing more. Well George wasn't badly hurt, in fact he*

*wasn't hurt at all of course and was able to walk back down the hill
with the rest of us, and so that was the morning exercise".*

This could almost have been written as a script for an episode
of "Dad's Army"! However following Dunkirk and then the
capitulation of France the threat of a German invasion was very real
and remained so for the next twelve months. So the Home Guard and
other national defence forces had a very important responsibility to
fulfil and they did so with enthusiasm and dedication.

There was also a secret army manned in the main by members
of the Home Guard or men who were in reserved occupations; the
majority of the recruits were farmers or farm workers but a number
included gamekeepers, gardeners, woodcutters and builders. The
primary requirement was for men who knew their local countryside
well and could be trusted. We now know more about the activities
of the Sussex units thanks to research undertaken by Stewart Angell
and his interviews with surviving members and much of what
follows about the Sussex units draws from his book *Secret Sussex
Resistance*.

The Home Guard Auxiliary Units were established in 1940 as
a direct response to the threat of invasion. Their purpose was "*to
investigate every possibility of attacking potential enemies by means other
than the operations of military forces*"; in other words sabotage and
hampering invading enemy forces by blowing up roads, bridges and
railway lines. Their life expectancy after an invasion was thought
to be just 2 weeks. There were 3 battalions formed- the 201st in
Scotland, the 202nd in Northern England and the 203rd in Southern
England covering Kent, Sussex, Hampshire, Dorset, Devon, Cornwall
and Somerset. The Sussex Regional Headquarters was at Tottington
Manor, Small Dole and the Sussex patrols were organised into West
and East areas; the West area patrols operated at Arundel, Clapham,
Goodwood, Hurstpierpoint, Small Dole, Stansted, Staplefield,

West Ashling and Wiston. The patrols operated from hideouts-operational bases- that were often constructed underground and usually had a separate observation post that was hidden in woods or thick undergrowth. In addition there were Scout Patrols for East and West Sussex that helped organise and train the individual Auxiliary Unit patrols. The West Sussex Scout Patrol was led by a Lieutenant Roy Fazan and comprised 13 men from the Royal Sussex Regiment.

In all the Sussex had 23 Auxiliary Unit patrols comprising 139 men which gave an average size of patrol of 6 men. One of the West Sussex men was Harry Frederick Moore who was a gamekeeper and aged 43 in 1939. He is not mentioned in the 1939 Register but in 1911 lived with his family at Ashurst Cottage, Ashurst Wood near Cowfold. He had also served with the Royal Sussex Regiment in WW1 so clearly had the experience and knowledge that was required for the Auxiliary Units. He has not been identified as assigned to a particular patrol but this is likely to have been the Staplefield patrol that was the nearest to Cowfold.

The Special Duties Organisation was a section of the Auxiliary Units whose particular role involved communications and spying. Both men and women were recruited in the main from people whose jobs allowed for movement around the area such as doctors, midwives, postmen, vicars and farm workers. They were trained to make simple intelligence reports and to pass these to a radio operator using a secret "letter box" which could be an old tin can, a hole in a tree or just placed under a rock. The radio operator was classified as an "out-station" whose whereabouts was kept secret by siting most of the radios in underground hideouts. The radio operator transmitted to a local underground control station operated by specially trained Auxiliary Territorial Service (ATS) women, called a "Zero" station, named because the station's code name was always followed by the code suffix "zero". Zero stations passed their information on to the Special Duties HQ at Hannington Hall, Wiltshire via direct phone line. Zero stations in Sussex were at Heathfield in East Sussex, and in West Sussex at Wakehurst Place near Ardingly and at Shipley.

Following the D-Day landings, the Special Duties Organisation was stood down in July 1944 and the Auxiliary Units on 30th November of that year.

* * *

In the aftermath of the Dunkirk evacuation there was clearly an expectation of imminent German air attack on Britain. At St Peter's school there was a growing concern about the safety of the children in the event of an air raid. There was no public air raid shelter in Cowfold and not all houses had either an Anderson or Morrison shelter. So on 5th July 1940 Mr. Quick reported in the school log that:

> *"During this week precautions have been taken for greater protection in the event of air raids. We have no shelter and being in the second line of defence and surrounded by the military forces, we are now very vulnerable. I have therefore prepared for the bagging of the Infants' and Girls' cloakrooms as an air raid shelter for the Juniors and have appealed for a shelter to the parents and friends of the school sending out 250 appeals".*

Then on 8th July:

> *"The response to the appeal has been very encouraging. The total amount received has been £25 today…Many of the parents have volunteered to carry out the labour".*

In fact the total finally raised was £63 19 shillings and 6 pence. And then on 13th July:

"The following Old Boys and Parents of the school have commenced to dig an air raid shelter for the children. The work is being carried out voluntarily by: M E Gander; P T Doyle; W E Sayers; G Moore; E Hedger; W Hedger; A Minihane; J Minihane; A Woolven; W Bidwell; L Jester; T Golds senior; T Golds junior; A Langridge; C J Etherton; C Belton; G Belton; F Smith; T Mills. The work was very kindly overseen by Mr Fred Fowler of Messrs Fowler Bros who has offered to advise the work throughout".

But on 19th July the work came to a grinding halt. Mr Quick reports:

"Today I have received the following letter from Mr Dudley Hoper which fully explains my reason for abandoning work on the air raid shelter. The shelter is now fully dug and the footing for the walls prepared. Owing to the generosity of Mr F Fowler I am able to return all materials bearing only the cost of transport. All donations and gifts will be returned immediately and this letter will be published in order that donors may know why the work has ceased".

And the log book carries the full transcript of the letter from Mr Hoper which reads:

"Dear Sir. I was surprised to learn of a serious trespass on the piece of garden ground to the west of the school premises. I refer to that slip of allotment garden which your school managers hire from me at a small annual rent in order to provide you with extra garden ground. This slip of ground is only let for garden purposes. I find that an air raid shelter is being constructed on and under it.

I was never consulted in the matter; but I immediately protested to the school managers from whom I learn that they are in no way responsible and indeed declined to sanction the formation of a shelter at all.

The County Educational Authority has forbidden the removal of the children from the school building in case of an air raid.

The safety of the children rests with the school managers subject to the direction of the Educational Authority.

It seems that you are probably the person who has acted, but without authority, to construct an air raid shelter anywhere.

If this is so and you have trespassed on my land I hereby give you notice to immediately cease the work and make good, both above and below the surface, leaving the land in its former state. If there be any trouble I shall instruct my solicitors to move in the matter.

Yours faithfully

John Dudley Hoper"

Ouch! And clearly Mr Quick was very much in the wrong, however much he had the children's safety in mind. Work on filling in the trench began that evening. However over the next few days further discussions took place including with the vicar who then intervened with the result that permission was given to build the shelter so long as it was removed after the war. And so the shelter was eventually completed.

Barbara Ross remembers the air raid shelter:

"We had to troop out and go across the playground down to that awful shelter which was cold and wet and dark, and wait. There were no windows, just an opening and a blast wall to stop any blast coming into the shelter. You just walked in and then felt your way along the wall to where the person in front had stopped and then so did you. There was always water on the floor".

Mary Matthews adds:

> "I can remember going in an entrance and it went all the way round to the other end where there must have been another entrance. There were forms along either side of the shelter and you sat more or less with your knees touching. It was semi-circular in shape with only a small entrance and you could only see the children who sat opposite. I remember it being dark and stuffy especially when you had your gas mask on and damp and smelly in the winter. We used to go into the shelter occasionally as a practice drill. We moved to Mr Quick's whistle. He used to time us going into the shelter and then you stayed in the shelter for a time. Then after a while he would say "All right now, back to the classroom".

The air raid shelter appears to have been used for real for the first time on 30th August 1940. Mr Quick records that:

> "The air raid shelter was used today during a very heavy bombing attack. The whole arrangements were carried out in orderly formation and the children in safety within two minutes. Air combats took place at high altitude".

It was to be used again several times during the autumn and winter.

Outside the village some of the houses built air raid shelters. Colin Rudling remembers one being built at the bottom of Woodside Close in Shermanbury where he lived, for the five houses in that lane at the time:

> "The houses got together and built the shelter from corrugated iron. They had beds in the shelter and I went down there a few

times when the air raid siren went off, which happened quite often. There was little chance of a bombing raid on Woodside Close but had there been an invasion perhaps it would have been safer in the shelter for a while".

Elizabeth Chase also recalls an air raid shelter where she lived in Shermanbury in her memoires *Reflections of Shermanbury...and more*:

"My grandfather had built a dug out for us to shelter in on the edge of the wood, made of solid clay. It must have been very difficult to make because of the tree roots. My memories of being wrapped up and carried to the safety of it at the age of five still remain. Later on he made another shelter using shaped corrugated metal sheets and then covered with the soil dug out during its construction. This type of shelter was called an Anderson; another kind of shelter which some friends had was intended to go under a dining room table and was called the Morrison- but it had to be a very big table!"

There had been sporadic bombing by the Germans during the Dunkirk evacuation and afterwards; the first high explosive bomb to be dropped on Sussex fell near Cowfold at 3 am on 29th May 1940. The main air assault by the Luftwaffe started on 13th August-*Adlertag* (Eagle Day) - focused on destroying the RAF and bombing airfields and ports in Southern England; this began what came to be known as the Battle of Britain. On that day German losses were 48 aircraft destroyed and 39 severely damaged while British losses were 13 fighters and 11 bombers destroyed in the air and 47 other aircraft destroyed on the ground. Much of the RAF's ability to intercept and attack the German planes was down to the successful deployment of radar and the ground-controlled interception network, called the Dowding system.

Overall *Adlertag* was a failure but this did not deter the Luftwaffe from continuing its campaign which lasted into September with heavy losses on both sides; attacks during this period included on Tangmere airfield on 16th August where 13 personnel were killed and on the Fleet Air Arm base at Ford where 39 personnel were killed. The real threat to the RAF was not the loss of fighter planes but of fighter pilots, either killed or badly wounded, with their replacements having little operational experience; in addition experienced pilots were now almost completely exhausted having flown often up to three sorties a day. But at this stage during August and in retaliation for a British bomber dropping bombs on Berlin, Hitler ordered the main Luftwaffe bombing attack to focus on London and away from RAF airfields with the first bombs dropping on London on 7th September; this gave the RAF some respite to recover its strength. The final attempt to destroy the RAF came on 15th September but again the Luftwaffe suffered very heavy losses. The immediate result of the failure to eliminate the RAF was the postponement by Hitler of Operation Sea Lion on 17th September, but not the final abandonment of the intention to invade Britain. Almost all the focus of attack turned now to the night-time bombing of Britain's main cities, in particular London, and industrial centres. This was the start of the Blitz which lasted until May 1941.

Throughout this period Sussex and its towns and villages including Cowfold were in the front line. Had Operation Sea Lion taken place, the German 9th Army would have landed between Bognor and Brighton and moved inland to form an initial bridgehead between Storrington and Burgess Hill as part of the total German bridgehead stretching from Portsmouth to Margate. After breaking out of the bridgehead the Germans planned to secure a line up to Reigate and across to Gravesend before pushing further inland as far as Northampton when it was expected the British would capitulate. So had the Germans succeeded there is little doubt that Cowfold and the surrounding area would have been overrun despite the efforts of the Home Guard and others to hold back the advance.

As it was the villagers of Cowfold and the surrounding area witnessed the fighting both in the air battles raging over their heads and in the German bombing raids which passed over the village on their route to London and back during the Blitz. Here is Bob Farren:

"I was in Cowfold when the Battle of Britain was being fought. It was great seeing all the dog fights. We boys all had our bikes ready and as soon as someone said "Oh there's one down at so and so" we were off to see if we could get souvenir bits before the police and the army got there. I shall never forget hearing on one occasion a terrible sort of ripping noise; I couldn't work out what it was until I also heard aircraft engines. I think it was a Spitfire although it might have been a Hurricane attacking a JU88 [the German Junkers JU88 was used as a heavy dive bomber during the Battle of Britain] *almost overhead and the noise of the eight 0.303in machine guns going off and firing ten rounds a second- it was a noise! I only heard it that once but I have never forgotten it. That JU88 came down at Newell's Farm, Lower Beeding. It made a fairly respectable landing and the crew all survived. I think one was injured and was taken to hospital; the other two were carted off to Horsham police station. We rushed up there on our bikes and there it was in the middle of a field on its belly although we couldn't get very near it. We also went to try and see another one that had come down at Hammerpond Lane- that was a Dornier that had come down in a wood. We couldn't get anywhere near that because it still had some bombs on board. There was another one in late 1940 at Broomer's Corner, Shipley. I happened to be outside the [Cowfold] churchyard in the evening and heard this aircraft that sounded as though it was really in trouble. It wasn't long before there was a rumble and a flash in the sky where it had*

crashed and blew up. I managed to get over there the next day and there were bits of wreckage everywhere. I remember coming across a large piece of metal lying in a ditch, lifted it up but dropped it quickly because there was an arm and a leg underneath it".

Bob also enjoyed watching the action at night:

"I used to come out quite a lot in the evenings when things were happening and watch the searchlights to the south and the flak in the sky. I remember one night hearing aircraft about and saw one being attacked by a night fighter; I can remember seeing the flash of the guns.

Another night I was outside near the lych-gate watching the action, thinking that if things started to fall I would dodge into the cover of the lych-gate, when Mr Quick came down he asked me what I was doing. I said I was just watching the action. He told me I shouldn't be standing around but I said that I could use the lych-gate for cover. Anyway he went off but came back later with a tin hat and told me to wear it".

Colin Rudling has similar memories: *"Watching enemy or friendly aircraft –fighters and bombers- overhead was more exciting than anything else. At night we would watch the searchlights searching the sky for German planes".* Colin also remembers a German plane machine-gunning The Street in Cowfold but no-one was injured. On his way to school he collected empty brass cannon shells from the dog fights overhead which had fallen onto the road and which he swapped at school. Jean Ross remembers picking up "chaff"- metal strips that German bombers dropped to try to confuse the radar- and taking the strips home to make decorations.

It could be very dangerous being caught out in the open whether just walking about or working in the fields. Mark Matthews had one experience as recalled by Mary:

"I remember my father working in the fields up the road with horses and an air fight taking place over the top of them and the spent cartridges coming down all around them. He had to come home because the horses were too frightened. I remember another incident when there must have been a dog fight, when my father said "Come out and watch this" and we actually saw a German plane, I think, burst into flames and saw the parachutes coming down through the flames. That was towards Lower Beeding".

Jean and Barbara Ross' mother was walking home to Longhouse along Pict's Lane when she was machine gunned by a German plane. She jumped into a ditch for shelter and was unhurt and did not tell the children about this narrow escape.

In all between July and October 1940 the villagers witnessed or heard about three German bombers that were shot down and a Spitfire and a Hurricane that crashed in the area. In addition 26 high explosive (HE) bombs were dropped in the area together with many incendiary bombs; these included 8 HEs and 2 unexploded HEs at Frithknowle on 25 September; 2 HE bombs at St Hugh's Monastery on that same night which wounded one monk and caused some damage (the Monastery was bombed a second time on 29th May 1941); 1 unexploded HE at Dragon's Farm; and 2 HEs and 1 unexploded HE at Frylands Farm. Bob Farren remembers hearing the bomb come down at Dragon's Farm:

"A bomb dropped at Dragon's Farm- I remember hearing that thing coming down; I was sitting at home doing my homework and could hear this thing rattling as it came down. It must have had a loose fin. I waited for the bang but there was only a dull thump. It went in deep but didn't explode and the bomb disposal people went to it and dug down to it and defused it but decided it

wasn't worth the effort of digging the thing out. To the best of my knowledge the bomb is still there".

Elizabeth Chase's grandfather was on fire watch duties at the Monastery during the first attack and told her that the Monastery appeared to jump up and down.

Mary Matthews remembers:

"my father coming into the house and saying to me and my Mum "Come out here and have a look" when the Germans were dropping incendiary bombs. I can remember looking up towards Kent Street wood and over to Cowfold and it was so bright you could read a newspaper. A lot of the buildings were on fire at Cooper's Farm".

And Pat Ferri recalls that:

"We had an incendiary bomb that came down about ten foot from the back yard [at Cotlands Cottages] and a plane came down in flames and crashed at Nuthurst all at the same time. I dug out the incendiary in the morning and all that was left was the fin".

These were exciting times for the children but a real worry for their parents and grandparents. The Battle of Britain may have been won and the threat of invasion averted but this was just the prelude to another nearly five years of further struggle and hardship for the people of the village.

Cowfold Village centre in 1939.

WEST SUSSEX CONSTABULARY

AIR RAID PRECAUTIONS

This is to Certify that   Frederick James FARREN.

of the West Sussex Special Constabulary, attended a series of Lectures on the above subject and on the   23rd.   day of   August.   19 38, he satisfied the Examiner.

Rank   Sergeant.

Division   Horsham.

Given under my hand and Seal, at Chichester, this   First day of   September,   19 38.

WEST SUSSEX CONSTABULARY
CHIEF CONSTABLE'S
-1 SEP 1938
OFFICE
CHICHESTER.

R.P. Wilson.

Chief Constable of West Sussex.

Air Raid Precautions training 1938.

National Identity Card 1939.

STATUTORY RULES AND ORDERS
1939 No. 1098

EMERGENCY POWERS (DEFENCE)
Restrictions on Lighting

THE LIGHTING (RESTRICTIONS) ORDER, 1939, DATED SEPTEMBER 1, 1939, MADE BY THE SECRETARY OF STATE FOR THE HOME DEPARTMENT UNDER THE DEFENCE REGULATIONS, 1939.

In pursuance of the powers conferred on me by Regulation 24 of the Defence Regulations 1939(a), I hereby make the following Order:—

Part I.

1. Subject as hereinafter provided, no person shall during the hours of darkness cause or permit—

(*a*) any light inside any roofed building, closed vehicle or other covered enclosure to be displayed unless the light is so obscured as to prevent any illumination therefrom being visible from outside the building, vehicle or enclosure;

(*b*) any light, not being a light in a roofed building, closed vehicle or other covered enclosure, to be displayed.

2. No person shall, for the purpose of advertisement or display, cause or permit any skysign, facia or advertisement to be illuminated, or any light to be displayed, outside or at the entrance to any premises or on any hoarding or similar structure.

Part II.

3. Paragraph 1 of this Order shall not apply with respect to any light the display of which is authorised under this paragraph by or on behalf of a chief officer of police in so far as it complies with any conditions imposed by him or on his behalf, or with respect to any light caused to be displayed by any member of His Majesty's forces acting in the course of his duty as such.

Lights in Roads.

4. Paragraph 1 of this Order shall not apply to the following lights for the guidance of traffic in roads:—

(*a*) A light in a traffic signal, provided that it is masked by an opaque disc covering the lens of the signal and having an aperture for the emission of light in the form of a cross having arms 3-in. in length overall and ½ in. wide and lying wholly in the upper half of the signal face.

(a) S.R. & O. 1939 No. 927.

Emergency Powers: Restrictions on Lighting 1939.

Mark Matthews at Wilcocks Farm during the 1940s.

Cowfold Home Guard:
Mark Matthews MM
and another.

Dr T. E. Matthews
Medical Officer
Cowfold Home Guard.

Jean and Barbara Ross at the site of a bomb crater in Pict's Lane 1940.

Vehicle Immobilisation.

Important Notice.

1940

To all owners of unlicensed vehicles in the South East Region.

Inorder to deny their use to the enemy should he invade us the Regional Commissioner has now ordered that all unlicensed private motor cars throughout the South East Region shall be immobilised forthwith.

You must remove the distributor head and leads and must also remove the carburettor or empty the petrol tank.

The parts so removed, and any spare parts of a similar kind belonging to the vehicle, must be labelled with the owners name and address and deposited with the officer in charge of the nearest Police Station.

Vehicle immobilisation 1940.

Aircraft crash sites and bombing including V1s around Cowfold 1940-1944

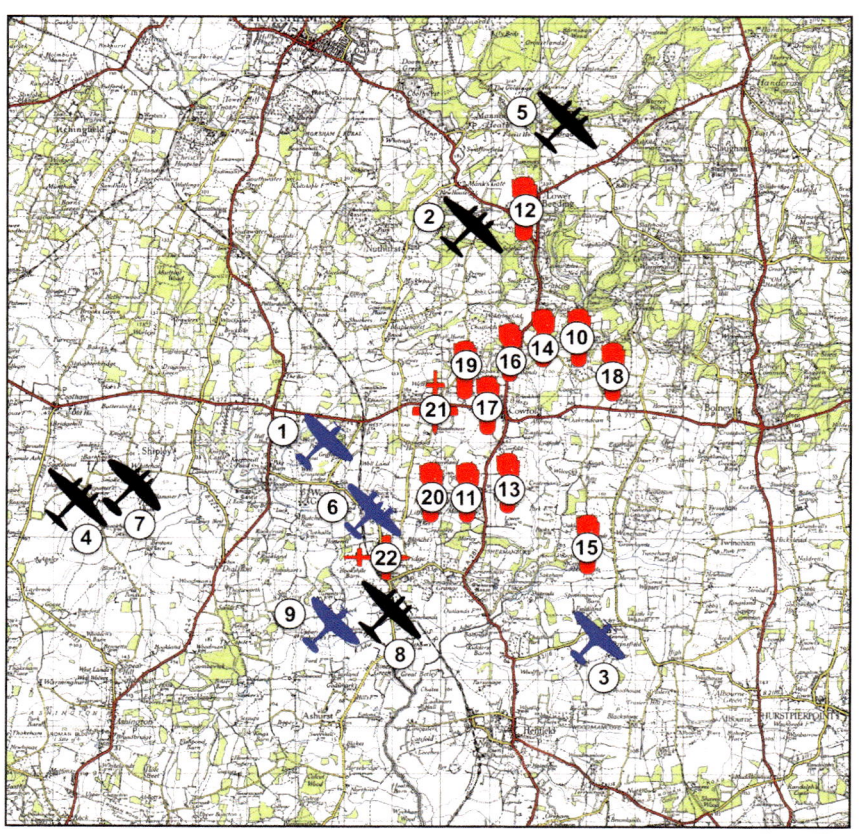

1. Spitfire forced landing in West Grinstead Park. 19/7/1940
2. Junkers 88 crashed at Newells Farm, Nuthurst. 9/9/1940
3. Hurricane crashed at Henfield. 1/10/1940
4. Junkers 88 crashed at Broomer's Lane, Shipley. 10/1940
5. Junkers 88 crashed at Lower Beeding. 29/10/1940
6. Beaufighter crashed in woods at Needs Farm. 13/2/1941
7. Heinkel 111 crashed at Smokehouse Farm, Shipley. 13/3/1941
8. Junkers 88 crashed near corner of Lock Lane and Bines Road, Partridge Green. 28/7/1941
9. Spitfire crashed at Sights Farm, Partridge Green. 2/10/1942
10. 8 HEs and 2 unexploded HEs at Frithknowle. 25/9/1940
11. 2 HEs and 1 unexploded HE at St Hugh's Charterhouse. 25/9/1940
12. HEs at Prongers Corner, Lower Beeding. 30/9/1940
13. 1 unexploded HE at Dragon's Farm. 5/10/1940
14. 1 unexploded HE at Frithknowle Cottages, Picts Lane. 9/10/1940
15. 2 HEs and 1unexploded HE at Frylands Farm. 10/10/1940
16. 2 HEs at Cowfoid on Horsham Road. 19/10/1940
17. 3 HEs and incendiaries at Cowfold. 28/11/1940
18. 3 HEs and 50 incendaries in Walhurst area. 30/11/1940
19. 50 incendaries at Capons Farm. 21/12/1940
20. HEs at St Hugh's Charterhouse. 29/5/1941
21. VI flying bomb at Clock House. 3/7/1944
22. VI flying bomb at Church Road, Partridge Green. 6/7/1944

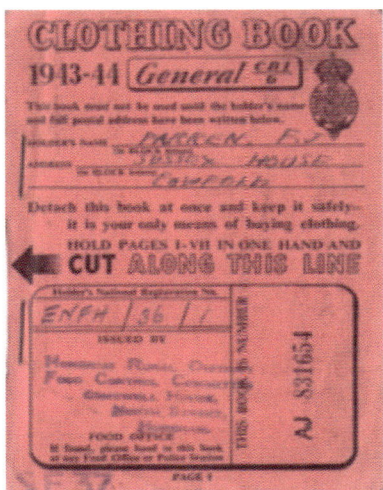

Clothing Ration book 1943-44.

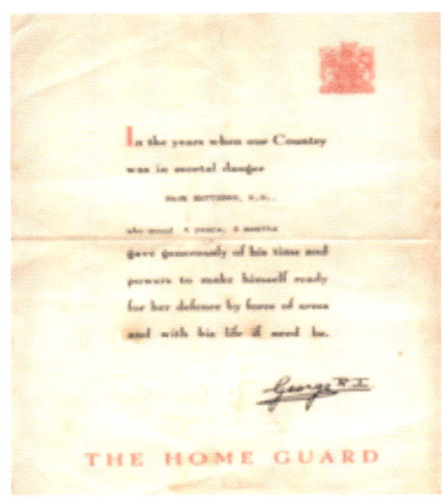

Mark Matthews' Home Guard commendation 1945.

COWFOLD

VICTORY CELEBRATION,

SATURDAY, JUNE 8th, 1945.

Programme of Events.

GENERAL COMMITTEE :

Chairman : Col. C. F. ASHDOWN, M.C.

Hon. Treasurer : Revd. W. B. SANDBERG, M.A.

Hon. Secretary : Mr. F. O. SPINKS.

Members :

Mrs. COLVIN, Miss L. PEACOCK, Miss H. PLUMBLEY,
Messrs. D. BOWERS, H. GOATCHER, S. FOWLER, D.
LAWMAN, R. H. P. QUICK, F. R. SLOCOMBE, R. THOMAS.

Price 3d.

A Lucky Number Programme Prize will be announced
during the Sports.

Cowfold's VE Day celebration programme.

Keep calm and carry on! 1941-1942

L ife at home was about standing firm in the face of adverse events and hardship and "carrying on". Daily life continued to be dominated by restrictions and shortages, about making do as best as possible with what was available. The continuing attacks on convoys in the North Atlantic caused a further tightening of rationing; clothes were rationed in June 1941 and led to the *"Make do and mend"* campaign launched the following year to provide housewives with thrifty design ideas and advice on reusing old clothing. Soap became scarce because its main ingredient was fat and that supply was affected by the continuing U-boat campaigns in the North Atlantic; in 1942 soap was added to the long list of rationed items. Even greater pressure was placed on farmers to increase cereal production and their efforts were controlled by increased surveillance by the War Agricultural Committees;

America's entry into the war in December 1941 following the Japanese attack on Pearl Harbour, meant that fewer American ships were available to import food to Britain and as a result farmers were ordered to increase wheat production by a further 840,000 tons. Pretty much every available piece of land was put to use to increase production. Milk production became a top priority and by 1942 milk sales had increased to over 1 billion gallons; to maximise human consumption of milk, calves were taken from their mothers very early in their life and fed on artificial milk. Timber was in short supply by 1942 (in 1939 only 4% of the country's timber consumption was met by local sourcing) and led to the formation of the Women's Timber Corps- known as "Lumber Jills"- overseen by the Ministry of Supply.

All of this was set against the backcloth of the progress of the war which during 1941 and for much of 1942 was not going well for the Allies. In North Africa British forces were forced back by Rommel's Afrika Korps to the frontier with Egypt except for the small enclave around Tobruk which was then besieged. In February 1942 Singapore fell to the Japanese, following the overrunning of Malaya and Burma; around 25,000 British troops were taken prisoner in what was considered to be Britain's worst defeat of the war. On the more positive side American troops started to arrive in Britain from January 1942 in preparation for the eventual assault on occupied Europe in 1944.

So whatever euphoria the villagers of Cowfold might have felt at victory in the Battle of Britain and the cancellation of Operation Sea Lion was soon dissipated by the daily slog of life under wartime conditions and the constant menace of the German bombing campaign and occasional attack by German fighter planes. Day and night-time bombing of London during the Blitz kept the village on constant alert. At the school there were regular air raid alerts during the autumn and winter of 1940, sometimes as many as four a day as on 2nd October when the children had to have lessons in the air raid shelter until the raiders had passed over.

Night time was probably worst for the children and their parents or parent. Mary Matthews remembers that:

> "We could hear the siren at Cowfold very clearly, even in-doors. That would sound whenever the ARP knew that the bombers were coming; usually it was quite early in the evening and then again at nine o'clock or ten o'clock or even later at night. It was a spooky sound but you were listening for it to go off- I was probably asleep but Mum was probably listening for it. Then you would get the all clear however long that took. The bombers would go overhead on their way to London, drop their bombs and then come back again. Sometimes they dropped bombs on the way back or maybe at specific targets such as Brighton. There were some bombs dropped in Kent Street wood and perhaps the Germans knew the Canadians were there. The bridge at Wineham was also bombed one day".

And Jessica Buxton and her mother had a particular reason to be worried:

> "My mother used to insist on sleeping under the stairs and she used to try to make me sleep with her and I hated it because I wasn't frightened. But the thing was you could hear the bombers going over and my brother Murray was with the Metropolitan Police in London in the middle of the Blitz. You could hear when the bombers started going over- horrible noise- and we knew that they were headed for London. You could actually see the glow in the sky when the raids were at their highest. And of course my mother was terrified for her son. That was awful".

The exposure to attack from German fighter planes is well illustrated by the following recollection of John Jones, living in Partridge Green, of an event on 30th November 1942 as recorded in "When the Whistle Blew"- the story of West Grinstead, Partridge Green and Dial Post during WW2:

"A crowd of us used to go from Jolesfield School to the recreation ground, take a football from the school, and play football. I was playing in defence with Bert Lander and Tony Sayers was in goal and the ball was right down the other end. They were kicking about their side of the pitch and I heard the noise of a plane, which you heard all the time during the war, and I looked towards Partridge Green and two planes were coming very very low over us. I used to know all the planes as I used to collect the Canadian postcards with pictures of all types and views on the back from different angles. I said to Bert Lander, "Look, there are a Messerschmitt and a Focke Wolfe coming." He looked up and I've a feeling he didn't believe me, and as it came over so low, the chap in the Messerschmitt dipped and I looked up and could see him looking at us and I could not believe it. He came over us and all the kids started running because he went round to attack the searchlight which used to be at the bottom of the hill up on the old windmill. They attacked that with machine-gun fire and us kids we ran and tried to get under the pavilion. I never forgot because it was on bricks and we were trying to get under it and there was broken glass, dog muck everywhere and half of us had to give up because it was so filthy under there. Anyway, apparently, I heard afterwards, it machine-gunned the searchlight battery but most of the men were down the pub as it was daylight. I don't know what damage was done. That experience was quite something, but they weren't interested in school kids. They went on from there and they shot up the train in West Grinstead station and killed the driver, and then they went on up towards Horsham. All of us kids were full of excitement going back to school, walking down the road, and over us came seven Mustangs, Americans from Ford or Tangmere, chasing after them. What happened after that I don't know".

The train driver who was killed was 67 year old George Henry Ansbridge.

Of course the threat of invasion still remained. Colin Rudling recalls:

"I remember one night my mum woke us up and the three of us spent the whole night in the bathroom in the dark. It was years later that I discovered the reason; my mum had heard trampling feet and heavy breathing and thought German paratroopers had landed; this was a real threat at that time, although I doubt the flimsy latch on our bathroom would have kept a paratrooper at bay for long. When dawn broke she discovered a herd of cows had invaded our garden. She must have been terrified at the time but none of this was passed on to us".

Pat Sayers remembers that her grandmother always kept a pot of pepper by the front door to throw at any German who was trying to get in!

Travelling outside the village was problematic. The whole of the South Coast was a very restricted and militarized area. Elizabeth Chase used to go with her grandparents to Brighton occasionally on the No 17 bus: "When you went to Brighton you got on the bus and you got as far as Patcham, opposite what is now the Black Horse, and you had to have your identity card with you and the ARP would come on the bus and check your identity card". Petrol rationing meant that there were very few private cars on the road as most had been laid up for the duration. Lady Barker at Longhouse had a little black coupé that she used very occasionally; her big car was laid up in the garage. But primarily travelling to the village from Longhouse was done by pony and trap. Petrol for essential transport such as deliveries of supplies was provided to ensure there was no interruption. For example Mr Tidey continued to pick up children for school and take them back using his coal lorry. And coal and wood were delivered to the school by the Shoreham Shipping Company and milk by the Arun River Dairy Company.

Travelling by rail was possible but the length of journey could be very uncertain due to bombing or other damage to the system; and on top of that all road and railway signs had been removed so as not to assist the enemy in the event of invasion. Elizabeth Chase used the train to get to her boarding school in Devon:

> "We used to travel by train to get to my boarding school- St Monica's- in Dartmoor, Devon. We crossed the fields to Partridge Green and caught the train to Horsham and then from Horsham to Reading which used to go via Guildford to Devon. It would take between 4 and 6 hours to get to Devon. Sometimes we went via Brighton and Exeter to Moreton Hampstead where there would be buses to take us to school. I used to travel with a label on my coat. It was a real experience travelling on the railways given the amount of bomb damage and delays".

And Jean and Barbara Ross used to go by bus and train to visit their grandmother in Westerham, Kent:

> "We used to go on our own to stay with our grandmother so we would get the bus from Haywards Heath, train to Redhill and then another hour's bus on from there to Westerham in Kent. Jean was in charge. There were no telephones so Mum would trust Jean to look after me. At that time all the road signs and the railway signs

had been taken down so there was nothing to say which station you were at. You had to recognise your surroundings and listen for the announcer to know to get off at Redhill. Coming back to Haywards Heath on the left hand side there was a big advertisement for Hall's Distemper- two big cut out men with a ladder- so you knew when you saw that that Haywards Heath was the next station. Bombing on the railways didn't affect us much but it did at Westerham where there was a branch line which was bombed".

Added to these difficulties was the ever-present blackout. It is difficult for us, who are used to ever-present electricity at the click of a light switch, to imagine now what life must have been like to live in almost total darkness during the blackout hours. Outside the house there were no or minimal lights shown and the few cars that were moving around had to have their headlights covered except for a small slit to allow some light to shine on the road. The frequent shout from ARP wardens "Put that light out" would have been part of the existence. But the villagers had to put up with these restrictions and it became a way of life as Colin Rudling remembers:

"Blackout curtains had to go up before you put the lights on and stayed up until it got light again. Did it make the house feel strange? Well we always had a fire and you got used to being by the fire and used to the blackout. We had electricity but we always had an open fire and during the blackout you wouldn't have the lights on anyway.

I never remember any ARP wardens coming down Woodside Close. We were surrounded by trees anyway. ARP wardens mainly operated in the towns and villages rather than in more isolated spots like ours. The policeman may have come down the main road, but he would have had a job seeing his way down our lane because there were no lights on.

It was quite exciting trying to get around in the dark, the depth of which is hard to imagine now when there are lights everywhere. In Woodside Close there were trees on each side of the lane all the way to the end, and in the summer on each side there were glow worms all the way down almost like street lighting; you'd go a long way to find a glow worm these days. And of course if you are in the darkness all the time your eyes get accustomed to it and you would see a lot more than people do nowadays because you never get true darkness now".

Bob Farren remembered the stars being so brilliant on a clear night because there was no light on the ground; the only lights were from the searchlights searching the sky for German bombers and from the occasional dim lights of a car. Out at Wilcox Farm, Mary Matthews remembers having to draw the blackout curtains as soon as it got dark and then having only candles to provide light. And Jessica Buxton tells of going to dances at Henfield and often having to walk back to Cowfold at night in the pitch black and the stars being so bright.

* * *

Another regular feature of life on the Home Front during these years was the continuous drive to ensure that nothing was wasted and that any surpluses went to help the war effort. One Sussex resident recalls that:

"Nothing was wasted during wartime. Our fathers used every part of the back garden for growing vegetables and many people grew cabbages and potatoes in their front gardens as well. Every type of fruit was gathered for jam making- blackberries, crab apples, even rose hips which made a nutritious jelly. All waste vegetable peelings were placed in a swill can for feeding to the pigs".

Another Sussex resident writing in a diary in October 1942 remembered that:

"All car owners with cars laid up are to fill in a form giving details of their tyres. There will be a big round up of rubber soon we imagine. Worthing has had a non-ferrous metal drive for a week. I took some decrepit coffee pots to the centre. We have a lot of collecting receptacles in the scullery now: one for waste paper and cardboard, one for pig food, one for compost, a jar for metal milk tops, another for bones and so on. Everyone is asked to have no more than five inches of hot water in the bath. Bread is a grey colour because of the flour. We are advised not to make Christmas puddings till much later as they get mouldy quickly. The few advertisements on hoardings advise us to do things like "Save more and lend it to the Government".

What this extract hints at is the enormous effort put in by various Government departments in particular the Ministry of Food and the Ministry of Supply to advise the people about contributing to the war effort or keeping themselves prepared for possible invasion which was still a threat at this time. The Dig for Victory campaign was promoted by a series of posters, magazines and films such as *"Dig for Victory"* made in 1941 and *"The Compost Heap"* made in 1942. War cookery leaflets issued by the Ministry of Food advised on food preparation and nutrition and extolled the virtues of consumables such as cheese and potatoes as well as providing recipes for making tasty dishes with ingredients that were not rationed as well as with those that were. One memorable non-meat dish was the "Lord Woolton pie" created by the chef at the Savoy Hotel in 1941 and named after the Director General of the Ministry of Supply; this comprised diced root vegetables, such as carrots and swedes, spring onions and a small amount of oatmeal and vegetable extract and put together with potato as a pie crust and oven baked (see Appendix D).

Radio was also used extensively to hammer home the messages. Television had been switched off for the duration on 1st September 1939 but in any event there were only 25,000 sets in use in the country at that time. Radio became the primary medium for mass communication and was available in most homes even though many had radios that relied on battery accumulators which needed to be charged up at regular intervals; Farren's garage in Cowfold was about the only place in the vicinity that would provide this service.

Before the war there were two radio stations- National and Regional. On 2nd September 1939 radio broadcasting was restricted to just the newly named Home Service which broadcast from 7 am to just after midnight with main news bulletins airing at 7.00am, 8.00am, 1.00pm, 6.00pm, 9.00pm and midnight; that was augmented by a Forces Programme from June 1940.

It is not possible to exaggerate the contribution that radio made as a means of promoting key messages, news and propaganda and also as a means of raising and maintaining morale. Exhortations about diet and nutrition and self-sufficiency were a constant feature of programmes such as *"In your garden"* with Cecil Middleton and *"Radio Allotment"* which went out live for 10 minutes every other Wednesday starting on 18th February 1942. News programmes and reports from war correspondents enabled civilians to keep up with the progress of the war and reporters such as Richard Dimbleby and Alvar Liddell and Ed Murrow for the American CBS became household names. And light entertainment came in the form of music programmes, some children's programmes, comedy programmes such as Tommy Handley's *"It's that man again"* which attracted an audience of around 40% of the British population, and morale boosting songs by various artists including Vera Lynn and Gracie Fields. Later in the war and influenced by the American troops, jazz and swing became popular as did the Big Band sounds of Glen Miller and others.

Propaganda was used both on the radio and via newspapers and posters to encourage the people to maintain their efforts to help the war effort as well as to lift morale. The latter often involved the use of exaggerated figures to claim a victory or minimize a defeat and was broadcast to the countries occupied by the Germans to bolster their morale and resistance. Of course the Germans used the same methods to try to undermine British civilian morale, the most notorious example being the regular broadcasts during the day by William Joyce, "Lord Haw-Haw", whose opening phrases *"Germany calling, Germany calling"* carried menace; although it was illegal to listen to him many people did, some taking his misinformation seriously but most regarding it as another form of light entertainment. Another example of German attempts to demoralise the population was a leaflet dropped near Petersfield in 1941 that shouted *"The Battle of the Atlantic is being lost!"* and went on to claim that all attempts to counter the U-boat and bomber campaigns had failed and that starvation was inevitable; that if the war continued until 1942, 60% of the population of Britain would starve.

Alongside the use of radio, films, magazines and posters to inform the public and make them aware and encourage their contribution to the war effort were the many information bulletins and official letters that were issued on a regular basis. Examples include the advisory leaflet *"If the Invader comes"* issued by the Ministry of Information in conjunction with the Ministry of Home Security in 1940 which listed six rules on how to frustrate the enemy and a seventh that made a final appeal to the civilian population which read: *"Remember always that the best defence of Great Britain is the courage of her men and women. Here is your seventh rule: THINK BEFORE YOU ACT. BUT THINK ALWAYS OF YOUR COUNTRY*

BEFORE YOU THINK OF YOURSELF". A similar leaflet entitled *"Beating the Invader"* issued in 1941 provided advice on what to do if an invasion had happened; this included advice on what it would mean if church bells were rung (bearing in mind that all bell ringing had stopped at the beginning of the war) - that was a warning to the local garrison that troops had been seen landing from the air in the neighbourhood of the church in question.

Another leaflet issued by the Ministry of Home Security in September 1942 as an update to earlier advice, entitled *"Objects dropped from the air"* described new types of German incendiary bomb, bombs combining high explosives and firepots, and phosphorus-oil bombs. And a leaflet issued by Horsham Rural District Council advised civilians what to do in the event that their water supply was cut off or contaminated.

For the Cowfold villager all of this including responding to the demands of rationing and blackout became part of the normal routine and life carried on as best it could. The general acceptance of this without seemingly little or no upset or disgruntlement helped to bring the community together in a strong sense of "we're all in this together" and as the motivational 1939 poster advised, *"Keep calm and carry on".* And by and large the people of Cowfold did exactly that.

A key role in maintaining order in Cowfold was played by the local policeman PC Albert Elliott. His daughter June Knight has kindly made available his scrap books of cuttings and written accounts before, during and after the war period, of some of the misdemeanours and other challenges that he faced. These included the theft of a bicycle by a Jack Matthews of Wisborough Green for which he was bound over for 12 months; working an unfit horse by James Greenslade of Woldringfold Farm, Lower Beeding and Arthur Savoury of Chatsfield Cottage, Lower Beeding both of whom claimed that they had no choice given the amount of work that they had to do- Greenslade was fined £7 and Savoury £1; failure to bury two dead sheep by Harold McIntyre of Brownings Farm, Cowfold who was fined 10 shillings; the theft of a bicycle at the Royal Oak, Wineham by a Canadian soldier in May 1942 for which the soldier received 14 days hard labour; and theft and housebreaking by a 14 year old boy who also admitted seven other offences and was sent to an approved school. In another case, Frank Sendall of Singers Farm, Cowfold was found guilty of receiving stolen bicycles and was sentenced to 12 month's hard labour. Another case that PC Elliott was involved with concerned a member of the Women's Land Army, Pearl Edwards, who was found guilty of stealing a handbag including 3 shillings and 5 and a half pence from Ann Murphy of Old Mill Cottage, Littleworth and cosmetics from Barbara Eggleton of Cooper's Cottage, Cowfold, while at a dance at Cowfold Village Hall; Pearl Edwards was put on probation for two years and ordered to pay costs of £1 10 shillings at a rate of 2/6d a week. And in November 1942 PC Elliott investigated the theft of Dr Matthews' Standard car- EPX678- by two soldiers which was later found at Seaford. The two soldiers gave themselves into custody for this and other offences.

PC Elliott also attended the sites of plane crashes in the area, not least to prevent young lads like Bob Farren from getting too close to the wreckage and taking souvenirs because of the danger of bombs or ammunition exploding. Among those he attended were the Hurricane crash at Drewitts on 21st April 1940 where the pilot, Pilot Officer Gordon Wilson was killed, the Spitfire crash in West Grinstead Park on 19th July 1940, the Junkers 88 crash at Plummers Plain on 31st August 1940, the bombing of the Monastery on 25th September 1940, and the unexploded bomb at Dragon's Farm on 5th October 1940.

* * *

Almost every day civilians were encouraged and reminded to make their contribution to the war effort and generally "do their bit". This took many forms including from being careful what they said in public ("*Walls have ears*" and "*Careless talk costs lives*"), to collecting and using or preserving wild or spare fruit, and to fundraising.

The Sussex resident quoted above referred to collecting fruit. For the mothers and children of Cowfold and the surrounding area, as for others in the country, this was a regular feature of life and was very necessary too because shortages or absences of fruits like oranges meant deficiencies of Vitamin C, a vital ingredient in a healthy diet. Rosehips and blackcurrants made into syrup were a good replacement for Vitamin C rich fruits and from September 1941 there was a concerted campaign to encourage boy scouts, girl guides and other school children to collect rosehips for processing; in 1942 333 tons were collected and this increased a year later to 492 tons.

A number of those interviewed for this book remember going out from school to collect rosehips which were sent off for processing into syrup. Mary Matthews recalls collecting "gallons" of them with her mother from around the farm and then taking them into school. Jean Ross also remembers collecting calf's foot leaves which were used for dressings because they contained a form of antibiotic. Fruit and vegetables were sent to food preservation centres run by the Women's Institute. These centres had been established and operated from the summer of 1940 and in that year 1,671 tons of fruit were preserved or canned.

Preserving foods involved both canning, a relatively new concept for the British housewife, or bottling. The WIs were helped by their Canadian counterparts donating them useful tools such as canning machines which could be shared out among the housewives. Preserving fruits and vegetables by bottling was largely done using Kilner jars. But a key ingredient was sugar which was rationed. So many housewives started saving up their sugar rations at the start of the summer to enable them to have enough by canning or bottling time. They were helped in some years of the war by the Ministry of Food doubling the allowance of sugar to encourage home preserving.

St Peter's School was at the forefront of Cowfold's contribution to this activity, including helping with the potato harvest. The following extracts from the school log book show how big a contribution the children made:

"2nd October 1941- The children have collected 15 cwts of vegetables to send to the Minesweepers on Tuesday morning and a quantity of rosehips. These have been sent on each Tuesday morning. An appeal for roseberries [guelder rose berries] by the Government Food Control resulted in the collection of some seven pounds today. These will be forwarded by the WVS for jam making as they contain valuable vitamin C".

"5th November 1941- There was quite a good collection of vegetables sent to the Minesweepers on Tuesday morning and a quantity of rosehips. Total weight to date is approximately 2 tons. About 10 lbs of horse chestnuts sent; these are very scarce."

"19th November 1941- Seven boys over 12 years of age have been employed by Mr Thomas [of Crateman's Farm] for potato digging at the rate of wage laid down by the LEA."

"15th May 1942- During this week the children have undertaken the collection of medicinal herbs and have to date collected 2 cwts."

"29th May 1942- 15lbs of nettles and 4 lbs of mixed herbs were sent to the centre today."

The children also responded to other calls for scarce items including waste paper; on one occasion in 1941 the funds raised from paper salvage by the children enabled a new radio and gramaphone to be purchased by the Sussex Regiment and given to the school. Paper was in such short supply that there was a concerted effort to reuse envelopes some of which could serve for three or more journeys; and materials used to package food items would also be used as envelopes.

There were countless various other campaigns to raise money to support the war effort as well as local initiatives such as whist drives. An early campaign to raise money for Spitfires started in May 1940 and during the Battle of Britain more than 1,400 appeals were set up, many co-ordinated by local newspapers which carried lists of individual donations. The BBC joined in, listing the latest successful funds and major donations at the end of news bulletins. At its peak the fundraising effort achieved an average of £1 million a month. In February 1942 a "*Warship Week*" was held and donors were invited to invest money either in National War Bonds, or Savings Bonds, or in Defence Bonds.

Although these were dark days when for much of 1940 and 1941 the country and its Empire was essentially on its own against the onslaught of the Germans and Italians and later the Japanese, the makings of what was later to be termed "Fortress Britain" were started not least by the arrival of the Canadians in 1940 and then later the Americans in 1942.

The Canadians 1940-1943

C anada declared war on Germany seven days after Britain but had mobilised on 1st September in anticipation of the outbreak. Canadian troops embarked for the UK in December and arrived in Scotland towards the end of the month, before moving to Aldershot where some 330,000 soldiers undertook training before taking up the defence of the UK while most of the British troops were with the British Expeditionary Force on the Continent. In September 1940 Canadian troops, predominantly the 1st, 2nd and 3rd Infantry Divisions, which together formed the 1st Canadian Army, began to arrive in Sussex, replacing the 3rd British Infantry Division under General Montgomery: the 2nd Canadian Division was deployed along the coast from Chichester to Eastbourne including the area around Cowfold, which also accommodated units of the Canadian 1st Division. Many units remained there until the D-Day landings in June 1944. They were not the only Allied troops in the area. Others included the 30th US

Division, the 4th Armoured Brigade, the 27th Armoured Brigade and the 15th Scottish Division but it was the Canadians who appear to have made a significant impact on the villagers of Sussex, including Cowfold; some 6-7,000 Sussex girls found husbands from the Canadian soldiers.

The Canadians were stationed and billeted in most of the large houses in the area but were also billeted with local families or in purpose built camps. Around Cowfold the forward headquarters of the 1st Canadian Army was at Knepp Castle, the 3rd Canadian Signals Division was at Shermanbury Grange, the 2nd Provost Company which provided the military police for the Second Division was based at Henfield, the 2nd Canadian Division was at Billingshurst and other units were at St Hugh's Monastery (a small detachment of Canadian Signals), Clock House (French Canadian troops), Ewhurst Manor and at Shermanbury Place (11th Canadian Army Tank battalion). A large camp was built along the Grove, the driveway leading off the Henfield to Cowfold road and towards Shermanbury Place and St Giles' Church; Elizabeth Chase remembers going through the camp: *They would be stripped to the waist doing their ablutions while their dinner was cooking. They were very friendly and very nice. In fact they built one of our air raid shelters for us using filled sand bags*. Another large camp was built in Kent Street wood and yet another was in the woods behind South Lodge in Lower Beeding as remembered by Jim Parsons. There was also a large camp at Monk's Gate on the road to Horsham.

For the early part of their stay in the area, the Canadians practiced for defensive manoeuvres in anticipation of a possible German invasion; later and up to 1944, and together with British, American and Free French troops, the preparations were for the planned landings on the coast of France on D-Day and the liberation of Europe. The villagers in the area would have seen or heard these preparations both in terms of the troop traffic through the villages and in practice attacks and other manoeuvres. Practice river crossings were undertaken over the River Adur near Ashurst, on occasion using live ammunition. And villagers going about their daily business could suddenly come face to face with troops emerging from the undergrowth as Elizabeth Chase remembers: *"My grandmother was filling a bucket with water from the outside tap when she noticed the grass move and a blackened face appeared which startled her; she discovered it was one of the Canadian soldiers on manoeuvres from the Grove crawling through a ditch"*.

The Canadians, particularly the English speaking soldiers, appear to have integrated quite successfully with the local villagers and to have been popular. Those interviewed for this book have good memories of their contacts with the soldiers. Pat Sayers was very young at the time but does remember the Canadians coming through Cowfold from Clock House in trucks or marching. Colin Rudling confirms this:

> *"A lot of them were on foot probably being trained up and hardened up before D-Day. But there were loads trooping through Cowfold village and they would stop outside the shops and buy drinks or people would go out and give them drinks. That was a daily occurrence building up to D-Day which became almost frantic the nearer that got"*.

Jean Parsons and Eric Vincent also remember them coming through the village and stopping off at the shops; they also remember the troops giving them cakes, chocolate and chewing gum. Eric's mother took in washing for some of the troops and Eric remembers them playing baseball at Clock House.

During their rest periods the troops quite readily mixed with the locals in pubs and at dances often put on for their benefit. Elizabeth Chase recalls that they frequented Mock Bridge House then owned by a Mrs Whelan and where Elizabeth's mother helped in the canteen. They would also have relaxed in the Red Lion and Hare and Hounds in Cowfold and in other pubs in the area.

The soldiers also used the public transport along with the locals. Elizabeth Chase again:

> "I can remember sitting on the bus once when the Canadians were there. I have an abhorrence of grass snakes which were always around here and this Canadian had them wound around his hand. So the Canadians used to use public transport as well".

Jessica Buxton, who was at a boarding school near Shrewsbury for much of the war, recalls the excitement of going to a dance at Cowfold Village Hall where Canadian soldiers were invited.

> "Coming home for the holidays if any of my brothers were at home then I was allowed to be escorted to a dance at the Village Hall. There were soldiers there and it was very exciting if you had a dance with one of them. And a lot of them were Canadians and that seemed to be even more exciting. But there was no nonsense because I was escorted by my brothers".

The Canadians were very generous to the children, as Colin Rudling recalls:

> "I did go to a Christmas party that the Canadians put on in the Partridge Green village hall and one at the old school in Shermanbury. They were really good; they had a magician and other entertainments. But the best part was that they gave us a present afterwards of a drawing book with an orange cover. That was gold dust; as a child I liked drawing and painting and we had no proper paper at all. Even at school we didn't have proper paper

and had to use wrapping paper that the sugar came in and cut up. There were no crayons and pencils were hard to get hold of. So to have a whole thick book of blank paper was wonderful".

Mary Matthews has similar memories of their kindness:

"The soldiers were fine to us. They used to give us different bars of chocolate with lovely outer coverings. We used to collect them. Every now and again they would lay on a variety show at the camp and they were very good. They had a big marquee there and they put forms down for us to sit on. All the locals used to go. There would be singing and dancing and they would do conjuring tricks- a really good variety show".

Bob Farren remembered a Canadian artillery sergeant, Cliff Walker, who was very good to the family by bringing supplies from their equivalent of the NAFFI; Bob thought that he may have had his eye on his sister Dorothy.

That generosity was reciprocated as much as possible by the villagers as Mary Matthews recalls:

"My mother made butter at the dairy and the Canadians loved butter milk. When the soldiers had done something wrong they were put on what they called "fatigues". They were put inside an enclosure that was surrounded by barbed wire netting where they had to do things like spud bashing. But sometimes the sergeant would march them down the road and they would stop at our farm, queue up at the dairy, wait for my mother to finish making the butter and then drink the butter milk. And then they would be marched back again.

My Mum got to know some of the soldiers because she took a lot of the letters in for them. I can remember one chap turned up –

I don't know whether he was stationed near us or not- but he was actually a cousin, although I never found out where in Canada he lived or how he came to be living there".

The training and preparations that the Canadians undertook were severely and tragically tested on the morning and through to the early afternoon of 19th August 1942. Operation Jubilee was an Allied assault on the German occupied French town of Dieppe. The raid's objectives were numerous including testing the ability to seize and hold a major port on the French coast, gathering intelligence and destroying German coastal defences, port structures and strategic buildings. In addition the intention was to lure the German Luftwaffe into an aerial combat with the RAF. And there was an added expected bonus of boosting morale and demonstrating to the Russians, the British commitment to opening a Western front in Europe to relieve the pressure on the Russians fighting on the Eastern front.

The raid was carried out by 5,000 Canadian troops, predominantly from the 2nd Division, 1,000 British commandos and 50 US Army Rangers, supported by tanks, the Royal Navy and a smaller force of RAF landing contingents. It is likely that some of the Canadians who went on the raid would have been known to the inhabitants of Cowfold and the surrounding area.

It was a disaster in terms of loss of life or wounding and capture by the Germans. Of the 5,000 Canadians who made it ashore, 3,367 (almost 68%) were killed, wounded or captured. The 1,000 British commandos lost 247 men. The RAF failed to lure the Luftwaffe into open battle, and lost 106 aircraft (at least 32 to anti-aircraft fire or accidents), compared to 48 lost by the Germans. The Royal Navy lost 33 landing craft and one destroyer. Virtually none of the objectives was met.

And yet there was a view that the lessons learnt from the tragedy were applied in the subsequent successful D-Day landings. Vice

Admiral Mountbatten who planned the raid later said: "*I have no doubt that the Battle of Normandy was won on the beaches of Dieppe. For every man who died in Dieppe, at least 10 more must have been spared in Normandy in 1944.*" That view was also held by Winston Churchill but was unlikely to have been shared by the relatives and friends of those who had been killed.

The loss of so many Canadians was felt keenly by the villages that many had come almost to call home, including Cowfold and Partridge Green. This was a clear testament to the affection that the villagers felt for the troops and to the extent to which the soldiers had assimilated to their English surroundings.

The tragedy of Dieppe did not of course stop the training and preparations for the greater assault on Europe that would come two years later. The Canadian 2nd Division was rebuilt and went on to play a prominent part in the Normandy campaign and subsequent fighting in North West Europe until the end of the war. Before that, however, the Allies had to ensure that the war was at last turning their way.

The tide turns
1943-1944

Although the Dieppe raid was a disaster, it did mark a turning point in the war in favour of the Allies who now went on the offensive after nearly four years of being on the back foot. In England the Allied training shifted from countering the threat of invasion to planning and preparing for the assault on occupied Europe.

Between 23rd October and 11th November 1942 the German Afrika Korps under General Erwin Rommel was defeated by the British 8th Army in the second battle of Alamein which opened up the opportunity the following year for the invasion of Italy through Sicily; this was the first major success against the Axis forces for over a year and provided a significant boost to morale. At home church bells were rung for the first time in three years, to mark the victory.

On 2nd February 1943 the German 6th Army was eventually defeated by the Russians at Stalingrad after a siege of nearly six months with the loss of around 200,000 men, the Germans' first major defeat of the war; thereafter the Russian Army went onto the offensive, driving the Germans from their territory and beginning the march on Berlin. The Russian victory at Stalingrad was the turning point in the war on the Eastern front.

On 13th May 1943 the Allied invasion of Italy began, launched through Sicily, leading to the Italian surrender on 8th September. The Allied forces included some units of the Canadians, who landed in Sicily on 10th July.

And on the night of 16/17th May RAF 617 squadron of Lancaster bombers led by Wing Commander Guy Gibson – later called the Dam Busters- successfully breached two major dams supplying power to the Ruhr valley using for the first time the "bouncing bomb" developed by Barnes Wallis.

Encouraging though these events were towards the eventual victory over the Axis forces, at home for the villagers of Cowfold and the surrounding area the wartime restrictions and shortages were relentless and if anything worse initially than they had been before. In 1943 Britain was close to breaking point. Heating fuel restrictions were introduced from 15th January under the Control of Fuel (No 3) Order which impacted on the ability to grow some of the vital nutritious produce. The increased losses of Allied shipping in the Atlantic in the first months of that year meant that there were more restrictions on food imports and therefore increased shortages and a tightening even further of rationing. In March the U-boat offensive reached its peak, with a series of major convoy battles which resulted in Allied losses in the Atlantic of 82 ships (484,000 tons). The seriousness of the situation was summed up in a later Royal Navy report: *"The Germans never came so near to disrupting communications between the New World and the Old as in the first twenty days of March 1943"*. April saw some respite but nevertheless the Allied losses in the Atlantic were still high- 39 ships (239,000 tons). One U-boat attack on a convoy at the end of April resulted in the loss of four tankers in three minutes followed by another three over the next six hours.

In May the situation improved for the Allies due largely to a combination of the sheer numbers of Allied ships at sea, Allied air power at sea, and technological developments in anti-submarine warfare. These allowed the Allies to gain superiority over the German U-boat campaign and to hold onto this superiority. Nevertheless Allied shipping losses during May still totalled 34 ships (136,000 tons) although the number of losses declined thereafter.

However the improving situation in the Atlantic took longer to have a positive effect on the food and fuel supply chain. For example the cheese ration, which had shot up to 8 ounces in July 1942, fell back to 3 ounces in May 1943. And in July 1943 rationing was introduced for tea (2 ounces), margarine (6 ounces which could be taken in conjunction with butter), and cooking fats (2 ounces, which initially could be taken as margarine if preferred).

And there was no relaxation of the requirement on farmers to produce more and more from the land. By this stage of the war just about every piece of available land had been turned into production. But such was the demand to increase production that the land was becoming exhausted and this posed a real challenge to farmers such as Mark Matthews, Benjamin Capsey and Reginald Thomas. Various fertilisers were available and were used extensively such as gypsum which was quarried in Britain, treated sewage sludge and lime. New compound fertilisers were developed and launched in particular *National Growmore* which is still popular today. Composting was also encouraged and various leaflets were available to tell the population how to do this. Surplus produce was put to alternative uses such as straw which was used to build storage buildings and accommodation. Another challenge to farmers trying to meet the demands of the War Ags was damage to crops and machinery by pests. In 1943 it has been estimated that £6 million was being lost through depredations by rats. Such was the problem that a number of Women's Land Army personnel trained as rat catchers.

Successful working of the land and harvesting was essential to maintaining a reasonable level of food supply. Shortage of labour was only partially met by the Women's Land Army. Since 1941 Italian prisoners of war captured in the Middle East were brought to Great Britain and were put to work on the land; before that POWs, both German and Italian had been sent to America and Canada because of concerns about their presence in the country in the event of a German invasion. Following Italy's surrender in September 1943, 100,000 Italian POWs volunteered to work as "co-operators" and were given considerable freedom and mixed with the local population; German POWs were not allowed out of their camps until later in the war. In the area around Cowfold, the main POW camp was at Billingshurst- initially Italian and later German- and Italians were transported from there to work on nearby farms or to help with ditch clearing. Colin Rudling remembers seeing a party of Italians:

> "We had a squad of Italian POWs digging and clearing out the ditch at the bottom of our garden. They were friendly. They sang all day long, scrounged some pastry off my Mum and they got some pigeons they had poked out of the nests and made pigeon pie. They were as friendly as anything- really nice chaps- but the bloke guarding them was terrifying. He had a revolver stuck in the top of his trousers, a scared face- I suppose he was an ex WW1 veteran- and he looked like a pirate to me. But the Italians were as happy as Larry really, singing away, and I don't think they would have been too happy going back to fighting".

Barbara Ross also remembers Italian POWs helping Benjamin Capsey with the harvest at North Farm.

Colin also remembers seeing POWs held in a temporary camp in the fields below St Giles' Church in Shermanbury:

"At one stage I imagine for a very short time there was a prisoner of war compound in the field between Ewhurst Manor and the church. It had like a deer fence around it- a 10 foot high fence- and was full of prisoners who may have been Germans. I don't remember ever seeing any accommodation there; there was just this compound in the field and they were all herded in there presumably as a temporary arrangement. It may have only been there a few days. We were told to keep away from that area".

Children had been involved in harvesting since the early years of the war but now this was stepped up. "Harvest camps" were set up under the orders of the Ministry of Agriculture in which adults and children spent part of their holidays helping to gather in the crops and root vegetables. In 1943 over a thousand harvest camps had been established in which around 70,000 children worked; and for most this was an enjoyable and remunerative way of spending time. Children also continued to be released from school during term time to help with autumn harvesting activity such as potato picking, as they had been at St Peter's School in the autumn of 1941. On 21st September 1943 Mr Quick recorded that:

"Application has been received and granted for 15 senior children to work at potato lifting for Thursday and Friday afternoons."

Clothing had been rationed since earlier in the war on the basis of a coupons system. Initially there were 66 points for clothing a year; this was cut in 1942 to 48 points and then to 36 in 1943; two years later it was down to 24. The amount of points required for each piece of clothing was determined by both the amount of labour that went into its manufacture and by the amount of material used. For example a dress could require 11 coupons, whereas a pair of stockings could require only 2. And extra points could be obtained for work clothes such as overalls used for factory work; extra points were also given to new mothers. Some items had to be purchased with money rather than coupons, for example second hand clothing or fur coats the price of which was fixed.

Of course if a child's mother was good at sewing there was less need for clothing coupons. Jean and Barbara Ross were fortunate:

"Clothing coupons didn't affect us so much when we were at St Peter's School because Mum was so good at making things. But later in the war we were both at secondary school in Horsham and there was quite a strict uniform requirement even though it was wartime. We had to have particular gym slips, blazers, two pairs of shoes- one indoor and one outdoor- and initially at least, a Velour hat for winter and a panama for the summer unless they were ditched in favour of just a beret. So coupons had to be used for those items".

Their experience was shared by Elizabeth Chase who remembers her aunts and uncles giving their coupons to her mother so that she could buy Elizabeth's school uniform.

Despite these continuing hardships, life for the Cowfold villager had by now assumed a routine and a normality that belied the difficulties and obstacles that had to be faced every day. It still was very much a case of "making do and mend" or keeping calm and carrying on but this was now a normal feature of life and was hardly noticed in particular by the children. For them each school day followed the pattern set by Mr Quick and his teachers but with some exceptions. Most of the evacuated children who had arrived in Cowfold in September 1939, including from the whole Croydon

School which had resulted in separate and in some cases shared facilities, had returned home with the threat of German invasion now considerably reduced and this allowed Mr Quick to report in the school log on 16th December 1942 that:

> "Representation has been made to the LEA that as there are but 9 Croyden children and there is sufficient room in the school, the services of the Croyden teacher be dispensed with and the children all taught in the school. The Village Hall would be required no longer."

And again on 15th January 1943 that:

> "Miss Hynds' [the one remaining Croyden teacher] return after three and a half years' work in Cowfold and half a term with our children was told to the assembled school. Her association with the school throughout the period of her evacuation has been one of pleasant co-operation and will remain long in the memory of those with whom she had come into contact. She has always been conscientious in her work whilst in Cowfold."

But that did not mean that for some of the evacuees the upset and difficulties caused by evacuation to an unfamiliar rural location had lessened, or that they had become settled since their arrival in the area. On 5th May 1943 Mr Quick records that:

> "Stanley Wright, an evacuee living in Wineham, came to the school but then left to catch the bus to London. His parents later telephoned the foster mother to say that he had arrived home. The boy had been sent to school and should not have left. [One wonders how he was able to do so and how this reflects on his teacher's and Mr Quick's vigilance!]. He is to return on

Monday. The boy has had 13 billets and has made four excursions to London since 1939."

Clearly young Stanley did not return to Cowfold as expected, and had no intention of doing so. On 15th May Mr Quick records that:

"Mr Hall the billeting officer from Shermanbury, visited to say that the billeting papers for Stanley Wright of Wineham, who left for home and is still remaining in London, have been withdrawn."

Other features of normal school life were regular visits by the vicar to take the senior class for scripture, Nurse Baxter for routine health inspections, the dreaded dentist Mr Brabazon, and gardening classes for the boys and cookery for the girls. The early months of the year saw quite a few cases of illness in addition to the usual colds and other minor ailments. These included diphtheria, scarlet fever, measles and influenza. Empire Day was celebrated as usual on 24 May. The Free Places exams for Collyer's School and the Girl's High School, both in Horsham, were held in the Summer and among those who gained scholarships was June Elliott, daughter of PC Albert Elliott. Displays of Physical Training and Country Dancing were given by the children to parents at the end of the summer term at which contributions were made towards sending educational books to Mr Slocombe who we have met in earlier chapters of this book, who was a prisoner of war in Germany. And at the end of the year a Christmas party, one of at least two, was organised for the children by Captain and Mrs Roberts, of Cowfold Lodge, in the Village Hall.

But "normal" life was still disrupted from time to time at the beginning of the year by the air raid siren and the need for the children to take cover in the shelter. On 10th and 12th February 1943

German bombers flew over and dropped bombs on Horsham during which time the children were in the shelter and again on 15th, 17th and 18th February. While the German bombing raids continued during this period, these attacks were more sporadic and did not have the destructive results of the Blitz two years earlier. This was because German air resources had, in the main, been diverted from attack to defence, the intention to bomb the British population into submission by conventional means had been shown to be futile, and by 1943 the Allies were now stepping up their raids into Germany and the occupied territories with increasingly devastating results; the intention was to wage an all-out offensive against the Luftwaffe and the German aircraft industry in order to gain air superiority in the run up to the invasion of occupied Europe. Operation Argument was undertaken during February 1944, the destructive highlight being "Big Week" from 19th- 24th February in which 3,800 American and 2,351 British bombers were in action dropping just over 19,000 tons of bombs and destroying or damaging 75% of German aircraft industry targets. The Germans lost 2,121 planes compared with the loss of 411 Allied planes. Some of these daytime raids and their aftermath of the damage to Allied bombers were witnessed by Colin Rudling:

> *"Later in the war when there were day time raids on Germany you used to see great blocks of bombers going overhead. I remember seeing mostly bombers – Flying Fortresses and so on- coming back flying very low almost at head height with one or two engines out and full of holes, staggering back and it was amazing that they could still fly given the condition they were in".*

* * *

The main focus of the Allied troops and air forces was now on preparing for the invasion of occupied Europe- coded-named

Operation Overlord- and this had a massive impact on the local population. Much of the following information about the build up to D-Day is drawn from *"D-Day West Sussex"* by Ian Grieg, Kim Leslie and Alan Readman.

Around Cowfold and elsewhere in Sussex, villagers witnessed major exercises involving Canadian, US and British troops and the noises of tanks, increased troop movements through the villages and the pounding of heavy artillery shattered the tranquillity of the rural countryside. The situation and the impact on the villagers of Sussex were summed up by General Eisenhower in his book *"Crusade in Europe"*, written after the war:

> *"...the southern portion of England became one vast camp, dump and airfield...Passenger traffic practically ceased and essential commodities were transported with difficulty. Construction of the great artificial harbours engaged the services of thousands of men and added indescribable congestion to already crowded ports and harbours...Sustained by the certainty that a decisive effort was in the offing and inspired by the example and leadership of Winston Churchill, people cheerfully accepted the need of using their own streets and roads at the risk of being run down, of seeing their fields and gardens trampled, of waiting in long queues for trains that rarely arrived, and of suffering a further cut in an already meagre ration so that nothing should interfere with the movement of the soldiers and the mountains of supplies we so lavishly consumed."*

These preparations saw the start of an influx of British and American troops into western part of Sussex from early 1944 which rapidly increased. As British troops moved in, most of the Canadians started to move out. For example Knepp Castle, which had been the forward HQ for the 1st Canadian Army, was now taken over by the 15th Scottish Infantry Division and the Royal Mechanical and

Electrical Engineers moved into Clock House. It may have been units of these Scottish troops that Jim Parsons remembers seeing:

"I can also remember some troops- I think they were Scottish because I seem to remember they had kilts- marching down Mill Lane from the east end towards the main road but I don't know where they would have started from. My Dad put a bowl of apples out for them".

Most Canadian units moved nearer the coast or into Kent. But some still remained at Shermanbury and around Kent Street and Longhouse. The British 27th Armoured Brigade moved into Petworth Park, the 4th Armoured Brigade moved into Worthing and towards the end of February 1944 the 30th US Infantry Division arrived in the Chichester-Bognor-Arundel area. Restrictions on civilian travel in the area were made even more stringent as the cloak of secrecy descended on the D-Day preparations, and the Home Guards units were placed on alert ready for instant call-out; they were given the task of guarding bridges, railway tunnels and helping military police with traffic control.

But Cowfold villagers still encountered the troops in their movements around the area as Jean and Barbara Ross remember:

"We remember the run up to D-Day in 1944. We were both at the High School so we were cycling home one day; we got back to the village in the early evening. Longhouse Lane is quite a long road that goes up to the high Weald so it is quite a steep hill. We always had to push our bicycles up the last bit before home and for quite a lot of the way the lane runs between banks. The Canadian troops had got as much of their equipment as possible packed in the lane while they were waiting and they were out of sight from the air because of the trees either side of the lane. So we cycled up the first

bit of the lane and then came to a complete traffic block; there was no way we could get bicycles through. So some of the soldiers came to see what they could do. What we decided between us was that we would go on foot up through the sandpit and through the wood out into the field until we came to the gate and they would pass our bicycles through - there were six of us so six bicycles.

I'm not sure whether it was the same time but there were certainly Canadian troops in the area, but I remember my Mum was over at the big house doing the cooking, and there was a knock at our door and there was a Canadian soldier who asked to fill his kettle. So innocently Barbara and I asked him in. Mum came back and I suppose her face said it all because I can remember he said "It's all right Lady, I've got daughters of my own!"

A critical prerequisite for a successful invasion of occupied France was to have air superiority and effective air cover. The western part of Sussex played a crucial role in achieving this. When war broke out in September 1939 there were three established military airfields in the area; at Tangmere, Ford and at Thorney Island on the Hampshire border. By early 1944 these had been supplemented by a further eight airfields and advanced landing grounds. Westhampnett outside Chichester was the first of these additional air bases and as a satellite to Tangmere it played a vital role in the Battle of Britain. Another was Merston also near Chichester which became operational in 1941. In all some sixty squadrons of the RAF and British Dominion air forces took part from West Sussex in the air offensive that was part of Operation Overlord. Two Royal Australian Air Force wings and three Royal Canadian Air Force wings, flying Spitfires, operated from Ford providing cover for the landing craft in the Channel and on the landing beaches and made sorties inland to prevent attacks by German bombers and fighters; three Free French squadrons, flying Spitfires, operated from Merston providing low level cover for troop-carrying ships and over the landing beaches; a Free French Spitfire squadron and an RAF Air Sea Rescue squadron operated from Shoreham to provide cover for the landings and escort for gliders carrying airborne troops; six Canadian Spitfire squadrons operated from Tangmere providing cover for the Channel crossings and the landings; four RAF squadrons of Typhoons operated from Thorney Island to attack German armour; and one RAF Typhoon squadron flew from Westhampnett to attack German strongpoints and gun positions.

Advanced Landing Grounds (ALGs) were planned and built from 1942 to provide additional and improved air support for the invasion landings. Twenty three were built in Sussex, Kent and Hampshire of which eleven were used by the Americans and twelve by the British. Four were in the area around Chichester- at Appledram, Bognor, Funtington and Selsey- and a fifth was at Coolham, near Billingshurst. Coolham ALG was the base for two Polish squadrons and one RAF squadron each flying Mustangs; all three carried out a range of operations including deep penetration raids in May 1944. Coolham was also the base later on for various Spitfire squadrons including a Free Belgian unit and one from the Royal New Zealand Air Force. Full details of the airfields and landing ground are provided in Appendix C written by Michael J Gething.

Very strict measures were taken to keep these preparations including the construction of artificial harbours for the landings- code-named Mulberry- as secret as possible to prevent foreknowledge by the Germans. Sections of the coast and the training areas of the Downs were completely closed to civilians although some travel was still possible. Huge concentrations of armoured vehicles all waiting for the green light to start the invasion of occupied France, hampered that travel but was nevertheless an amazing and exciting spectacle in particular for children. Bob Farren remembered some of these sights:

"I can remember going along what is now the Crawley by-pass and all around there it was absolutely stiff with tanks, guns and lorries. I also had a bus ride out as far as Maresfield in late May 1944 when my sister was nursing at Tunbridge Wells and between Cowfold and Maresfield there was an almost unending line of trucks, tanks and guns".

Bob also remembered extensive aircraft activity:

"There were always aircraft about. I can remember seeing Dakotas flying over the village towing gliders on training exercises. I can remember seeing one American Flying Fortress coming back relatively low with bits hanging off it; it had obviously had a rough time and was badly shot up. I think he probably made it as far as Dunsfold airfield".

Jean and Barbara Ross recall that:

"We saw convoys of troops going through the village. One of the times when we were coming home there was a large convoy of motor bikes so we had to stop and it was the King and Queen although we don't know where they were going".

A very significant event, as recorded by Colin Rudling in West Grinstead and Partridge Green History Societies' book *"When the Whistle Blew"* was Operation Sidecar. This was an American practice operation for landing gliders as part of the preparations for D-Day. On 18th April 1944 48 gliders landed in the fields between Dial Post and Hooklands Lane, a site chosen because of its close similarity to the countryside found in Normandy. The force consisted of eight British built Airspeed "Horsa" gliders and forty smaller American Waco CG-4A Hadrian gliders taking off in four flights at 15 minute intervals. Each Horsa carried a jeep and a 57mm gun or howitzer or a similar weight of ammunition; twelve of the Hadrians were loaded similarly, while the others were loaded with sandbags to simulate a normal cargo. No troops were on board, only the pilot and co-pilot, in order to minimise casualties.

Forward weather forecasts provided General Eisenhower with a window between 5th and 7th June when conditions appeared favourable for the landings on selected Normandy beaches. On 26th May Eisenhower determined that the invasion should take place on 5th June. From that moment all camps in the Concentration and Marshalling Areas which had been made ready for some time for D-Day, were sealed allowing assault troops to be fully briefed on their D-Day roles.

May 1944 had seen glorious weather which helped the preparations. As the month came to an end and for the first few days of June the final convoys of troops made their way from Concentration to Marshalling and then Assembly areas in the Channel, leaving from Newhaven, Shoreham, Portsmouth and Southampton. The designated Normandy beaches were Utah and Omaha for the Americans and Gold, Sword and Juno for the British and Canadians, the latter for the 3rd Canadian Infantry Division and 2nd Canadian Armoured Brigade. But Ist June dawned dull and cloudy and weather conditions over the Channel were deteriorating. Over the next 48 hours the weather worsened still leading Eisenhower to postpone the invasion by one day. On 5th June the weather forecast looked more favourable giving a window of reasonable weather on the 6th and for a few days after before the next period of unsettled weather arrived. Eisenhower took the decision to start the invasion on Tuesday the 6th.

Such was the security around the last preparations for D-Day that for the villagers of Cowfold and the surrounding area it was almost as though one day the Canadians and other troops were in their various camps and the next and almost overnight they had gone. Colin Rudling recalls:

"As children we could roam anywhere; we were out and about and just disappeared off into the fields and woods. The Grove was not far over the fields from Woodside Close and one day it was absolutely packed with tanks and guns all parked up under the trees and camouflaged and then overnight they moved down to the coast and were gone".

And that is confirmed by Jean Ross:

"In the days before D-Day the Canadian troops went down to the coast ready to go across to France and they seemed more or less to vanish from the area overnight. I think the next morning after they had gone we didn't have any difficulty cycling down the lane".

And here is Mary Matthews on the same subject:

"Then just before D-Day they were gone. We didn't know when they went or where to. The site of the camp [in Kent Street woods] *was just empty".*

It is unlikely that the villagers in and around Cowfold got much if any sleep during the night of 5th/6th June. Aerial activity built up from midnight with bombers on their way to France. Then at 2.30 am on 6th June the airborne invasion of glider-towing aircraft passed overhead along with whole phalanxes of Allied aircraft: Dakotas, Fortresses, Lancasters, Mosquitos, Mustangs, Spitfires, and Typhoons. Bognor, Littlehampton and Worthing were directly under the flight paths of the British 6th Airborne Division, as was Cowfold.

At around 6.30 am the Allied troops started landing on the Normandy beaches at the beginning of what has been described as "The Longest Day". The American landing craft aiming for Utah and Omaha beaches were blown east of their intended positions by strong winds and had to land at more heavily defended places; American casualties were heaviest at Omaha with its high cliffs. The British and Canadians had better success at Gold, Juno and Sword beaches clearing several fortified towns and disabling two major gun emplacements at Gold using specialised tanks. But the Allies failed to achieve any of their goals on the first day. Only two of the beaches (Juno and Gold) were linked on the first day, and all five beachheads were not connected until 12th June. However, the operation gained a foothold which the Allies gradually expanded over the coming months. German casualties on D-Day have been estimated at 4,000 to 9,000 men. Allied casualties were at least 10,000, with 4,414 confirmed dead. Among those killed during the Normandy landings was Jean and Barbara Ross' youngest uncle:

"What really brought the war home to us was that Mum's youngest brother who was only six years older than me, was killed on the Normandy beaches- he was 19 years old. It must have been when they were supplying the troops and the ship was blown up by a mine. He was like a big brother to us".

The Normandy landings were the result of the largest amphibious invasion in history- code-named Operation Neptune-, were the exemplar of military and naval planning and were the overture to the opening of the western front of the Allies' attack on Germany which with the Russian attacks from the east saw the final defeat of the Third Reich 11 months later. And yet, amazingly, Mr Quick made no mention at all of this momentous day in the St Peter's School log book despite the screaming newspaper headlines that appeared that morning. So we are left to speculate on what he, his staff and the children thought and did to mark this important day.

Instead among the daily routine of the school, he records the school's contribution to *"Salute the Soldier"* Week starting on 10th June which was aimed at setting a monetary target to raise sufficient money to support the troops. Over the week the school children raised £82 10 shillings and sixpence. Colin Rudling remembers this campaign:

> *"There was an articulated cut out of a soldier with a tin hat whose arm rose up to a salute when you put in a penny. I don't know how much it took for him to salute- probably a pound. We imagined that when he saluted you had bought a tank or a Spitfire or something like that".*

If anyone in Cowfold thought that D-Day and the subsequent advances of the Allied forces would alleviate the threat of German aerial attack on the country they were sadly mistaken. For now Hitler launched the first of his Vergeltungswaffe- Vengeance Weapons- the V1 flying bomb designed for terror bombing London. And Cowfold and the surrounding countryside were again in the flight path of many of these pilotless bombs.

The lights go on again 1944-1945

T he V-1 flying bomb- or Doodlebug to give it one of its nicknames- was developed by the Germans at the Peenemunde research centre in 1939 but was not launched in earnest against England until 1944. It and its use as a terror weapon was known about by the Allies for at least a year before the first doodlebug was launched and as part of the pre-D-Day operations as well as after D-Day, the Allied bombers targeted the research centre and launch sites where these could be found. From July 1944, V-1s were also launched from bombers flying over the North Sea.

The first V-1 was launched at London on 13th June 1944, one week after (and prompted by) the D-Day landings. At the peak of the campaign, more than one hundred V-1s a day were fired at south-east England, decreasing in number as sites were overrun until October 1944, when the last V-1 site in range of Britain was overrun by Allied forces. In all 13,000 V-1s were launched at England but only around 2,600 actually exploded near their intended target; that was largely down to effective air defences which included anti-aircraft guns and interceptor fighter planes, and to the strategic bombing of V-1 launch sites and underground storage depots. The damage to housing in London - around 1.2 million homes destroyed- was nearly comparable to the Blitz nearly four years earlier but the casualty rate was lower- nearly 24,000 civilians killed or injured compared to 92,600 during the Blitz.

But the V-1 was more effective as a psychological weapon; it was called a terror weapon for good reason. It was an early form of cruise missile and arrived just when the civilian population thought that their exposure to aerial warfare had passed and when they were becoming very war weary. It exerted maximum psychological effect simply by the sound of the engine cutting out when it had reached the limit of its range and then falling silently to earth before exploding; no-one at the receiving end could be certain where the bomb would fall and therefore whether it would fall on them.

Jean Ross remembers this feeling of dread:

"I can remember very vividly we had Dorothy and Frank staying with us; I must have been thirteen at the time. I think it must have been early evening and Barbara and Dorothy were downstairs having a bath. I was in our bedroom on my own and heard this doodlebug and actually saw it going behind the trees. Then I heard the engine stop and I remember thinking "Someone might die in the next few minutes". In fact they didn't and the doodlebug crashed at Warninglid, just below the Half Moon pub. We cycled up to see it. But I can remember now that horrible feeling of doom. Psychologically they were a very effective weapon".

Jean Parsons had a similar experience:

"My most vivid memory of fear is when the first doodlebugs came over. We walked up to the allotments because Dad had one there and Mum was talking to these people and they were talking about the doodlebugs, and one of them said "Well I think it's the end, we're finished now." And I remember being very frightened then. We lived where we could look out towards the Downs over the Monastery and we used to sit there and watch the doodlebugs coming over, hoping that the engine wouldn't stop".

And here is Colin Rudling:

"The only time that I really felt fear was when the doodlebugs came over. As I was a bit older I realised, I suppose, that one could drop on my head. They had such a sinister sound and flew low; we knew the sounds of German and British planes but this was different. They would come over low and then the engine would cut out and there was a pause before they hit the ground and exploded. Even now when I hear a recording of a doodlebug, when it cuts out I still feel my heart miss a beat. One came down near the church [in Partridge Green] and that night I was sleeping at my grandmother's house around 400 yards away, and the blast blew off the curtain rail and the curtains in the room I was sleeping in".

Most of the V-1s flew over Cowfold to come down and explode elsewhere or to be shot down; they were tracked by Bob Farren's father and other members of the Royal Observer Corps at their headquarters behind the Drill Hall in Denne Street, Horsham using the code word "Diver". However there were three confirmed crashes and explosions around Cowfold and Partridge Green as recorded by the West Sussex Action Officers' Minute books- a detailed record of all the bombings, aircraft crashes and other serious incidents in the area during the war. The first at 7.15 on the morning of 3rd July exploded in the vicinity of Clock House and as Eric Vincent recalls, the V-1 was caused to crash by being tipped over by either a Spitfire or a Hurricane; this was also witnessed by Pat Ferri who felt the blast from the explosion. The Action Officers recorded that there was blast damage to Clock House and two minor casualties among the soldiers billeted there. PC Elliott attended this incident and recorded that one of the casualties was Driver L. O. Gladwin from 756 Company Royal Army Service Corps who was badly cut over his left eye.

The second was on the same day at 3.17 in the afternoon and caused damage to two houses near Cowfold- which ones is not recorded. It was believed that the V-1 was hit by anti-aircraft fire and lost height before crashing and exploding in hilly ground leaving a crater 20ft by 5ft; this may have been in the area around Pict's Lane.

A third incident was the V-1 that crashed and exploded at 3.45 am on 6th July in a field almost opposite St Michael's Church, Partridge Green leaving a crater 13ft wide and nearly 7ft deep. Two bungalows were badly damaged and there was slight damage to the church and to Jolesfield House but there were no casualties. This is the incident that Colin Rudling refers to above.

An immediate effect of these terror weapon attacks was another evacuation from London and other targeted cities, but this time on a smaller scale to 1939. Between February and November 1944, 21 children from different parts of London and 1 child from Portsmouth were admitted to St Peter's School with ages ranging from 5 to 12. About half were girls and among the evacuees were some brothers and sisters including John and George Talbot from Brockley SE15, Anne and Ruth Parkes from Clapham, Joan and Hazel Pummell from Fulham and David and Beryl Steer from Croydon. Unlike the 1939 evacuation their stay in Cowfold was short term- most had returned home by the autumn of 1944 with a few staying until after the end of the war. They were billeted in various houses in Cowfold and the surrounding area and in Wineham. David and Beryl Steer stayed for just over a year with William and Alice Sayers at 4 Council Cottages; Anne and Ruth Parkes stayed for 16 months with the Hornungs at "The Ivories"; and Joan Hillsdon from Hammersmith and Margaret Willett from Fulham stayed for 13 months with Percy and Francis Medhurst at "Woodville" on the Henfield road. Some of the evacuees were more fortunate than others. The St Peter's School log records that on 6th July 1944:

> *"The Welfare Officer visited the school to see Amy Foster, an evacuee who is in need of clothing and whose parents have just been found after several months' enquiry. A message was received this morning that her mother will send shoes for the child."*

Among the evacuees from London was the headquarters of the Women's Land Army which had moved to the capital from Balcombe Place, Haywards Heath the home of its honorary director, Lady Gertrude Denman but now returned to Sussex.

From September 1944 a new terror weapon was launched by the Germans targeting first London and then Antwerp and Liege as the Allied forces moved further into occupied Europe. The V-2 was the world's first long-range guided ballistic missile and was developed as retaliation for the Allied bombings against German cities. Over the following six months 1,358 V-2s were launched at London, 43 at Norwich and 1 at Ipswich; an estimated 2700 civilians were killed in the London attacks with another 6500 injured. The last V-2 fired at England killed a civilian in Orpington, Kent on 27th March 1945.

The psychological effect of the V-2 was considerable and significantly greater than the doodlebug. It travelled faster than the speed of sound, took approximately 45 seconds from launch to reach London and gave no warning before impact; so no-one in

Cowfold ever saw or heard a V-2 fly overhead. There was no effective defence against the weapon. Therefore the impact on the outcome of the war does not bear thinking about had the Germans been able to deploy this weapon earlier.

Despite the threat of the V-1s life for the Cowfold villager continued in its daily and unchanged routine. Rationing continued unabated and the community continued to pull together to help each other out when necessary while all the time listening to the news on the radio or reading the newspapers for updates on the progress of the German withdrawal from the occupied territories in the face of Allied attacks. Rome was liberated on 5th June 1944 followed by Paris on 25th August 1944. The Western Allies crossed the river Rhine into Germany on 22nd March 1945. Mark Matthews had been following the war's progress since the start on a big map in his house at Wilcox's Farm and was now able to plot the Allies' successes and setbacks.

However for him and for other farmers in the area the priority remained to maintain if not increase the production of cereals and root vegetables from the land as well as contributing to the supply of milk. Farmers were also central to the preparations for D-Day and after, by turning some of their land over to growing flax for ropes, parachute harnesses and for linen and canvas; by 1944 60,000 acres of land was used for this purpose. The pressure on farmers was intense, not helped that in the run up to D-Day the military had taken over 11 million acres of land for camps and temporary airfields. The demands of supplies from the factories meant that more women were drafted in for factory work rather being available to work on the land. And by 1945 the land was becoming exhausted and food production was starting to fall. The priority given to cereal and root vegetable production had meant a decline in the amount of livestock and therefore a resulting decline in available manure; farmers were now required to find alternatives to improve the fertility of the land.

One consequence of this situation was the increasing use made of German prisoners of war. Unlike Italian POWs who were used on the land from 1941, the Germans were held in camps until the threat of invasion had effectively passed. Now they were required to help with production from the land wearing a distinctive uniform of British army khaki dyed purple brown with lighter coloured red patches on the back and diamond shaped patches on the trousers. By 1945 58,000 POWs were working on farms or in commercial gardening operations. Some of those interviewed for this book remember German POWs working on the farms in the Cowfold or Partridge Green areas- for example Colin Rudling remembers Germans working at Lock Farm west of Partridge Green- either during the war or for a few years after war ended. In the country as a whole in December 1946, 19 months after VE Day there were 355,200 German POWs and by March 1948 there were still just over 82,000.

In addition there was still encouragement for school children to help with harvesting. Mr Quick records that on 20th September 1944:

"Permission granted for the afternoon session to commence at 1.00pm and finish at 3.15pm in order that seniors might assist in the collection of potatoes at Wallhurst Farm for the afternoon to clear the ground."

* * *

By the beginning of 1945 it was clear that the defeat of Germany was just a matter of time. The security and defences at home were being relaxed not least with the disbandment of the Home Guard on 31st December 1944. Male members were rewarded with a certificate signed by the King. That given to Elizabeth Chase's grandfather, James Frederick Ferdinand, reads:

"In the years when our country was in mortal danger
   James Frederick Ferdinand
   Who served 4 years and 6 months gave generously of his time
and powers to make himself ready for her defence by force of arms
and with his life if need be.
   George RI"

Areas of the coast and surrounding country that had been cordoned off to civilians were now gradually made more accessible. But daily life under the various restrictions, including rationing, continued as before. So did the need to maintain the supply of home grown food with much the same contributions being made by the children of St Peter's School.

Life was made significantly worse in January 1945 by the appalling weather. Mr Quick at the school records that on 10th January, Assembly had to be abandoned because of heavy snowfall. Again on 12th January there were very heavy falls of snow and that continued for much of the rest of that month. On 23rd January the roads were covered by four inches of snow and on 26th January the outside toilets at the school were frozen and water had to be carried to flush the pans. Many children and some teachers, including Mr Quick, came down with influenza and heavy colds. Then a rapid thaw in early February resulted in heavy flooding in the area. Snow fell again on 30th April and Mr Quick recorded that this was the heaviest snowfall and the latest in the year since 1908.

However the end of the war in Europe was now very close and events leading up to that happened quickly. Berlin was attacked by the Russian army on 16th April 1945, Mussolini was captured and executed by Italian partisans on 28th April, Hitler committed suicide on 30th April and Berlin fell on 2nd May. Also on 2nd May German forces in Italy surrendered.

Preparations at home were now being made for V-E- Victory in Europe-Day with a Government Circular 119/1945 issued on 2nd May about the arrangements at schools. It read:

"If the proclamation takes place while school is in session or is about to begin, the school should continue in session for the rest of the day. The two following school days should be taken as a school Victory Holiday, irrespective of the intervention of the week-end".

Two days after that circular was issued German forces in the Netherlands, north-west Germany and in Demark surrendered to General Montgomery at Luneburg Heath, east of Hamburg. On 7th May the remaining German forces unconditionally surrendered at Allied Headquarters in Rheims, to take effect the following day, so bringing the European conflict to an end.

On 8th May Mr Quick wrote:

"The news of unconditional surrender was announced at 8.25am on the Forces wavelength and official instructions were given by the BBC that children would not therefore attend school for VE+1 or VE+2 days. School has been closed for general thanksgiving."

V-E Day was a scene of massive celebrations across the country. Over one million people celebrated in the streets and in London crowds massed in Trafalgar Square and up the Mall to Buckingham Palace where the King and Queen and Winston Churchill appeared on the balcony. Churchill also appeared on the balcony of one of the Government departments in Whitehall to cheering crowds. In the country's towns and villages there were street parties, bonfires, church bell ringing and masses of waving flags and bunting.

But how did Cowfold celebrate apart from the school children having a two day holiday? It was interesting that of all eleven people interviewed for this book only one- Pat Sawyer (Ferri) - vaguely remembered a fancy dress ball as part of a celebration. There must have been a more significant event after six years of hardship and struggle.

And there was. Thanks to PC Albert Elliott's scrap book provided by his daughter June West we know now that a whole day- Saturday 8th June- was given over to celebrating V-E Day. The organising committee was chaired by Colonel C. F. Ashdown MC, the Treasurer was the Reverend Sandberg and the Secretary was Oliver Spinks. Committee members included Mr Quick, Mr Goacher, Mrs Colvin, Mr S Fowler and Miss L Peacock.

The day started at 10.30 am with a parade of members of the British Legion, Army Cadets, Fire Service, Girl Guides, and Women's Land Army in the School playground who then marched through the village to the church. A service of thanksgiving was followed at 2.30pm by sports events held on the Cricket Ground; sports included running races for various age groups, egg and spoon races, and a 100 yards race for men and women over 25 years old. There was also an obstacle race for men only, a sack football match between the British Legion and Cadets, and a tug-of-war with four teams representing north, south, east and west Cowfold and judged by Captain Lovett-Cameron RN. Side shows included *"The Lucky Bucket"*, a treasure hunt, skittle alley, Hoopla, darts, Guessing the name of the doll (presented by Mrs Sayers) and Guessing the weight of the cake (presented by Mrs Plumbley)- it is interesting to speculate how big this could have been given rationing! Children's entertainment was provided in the Marquee on the Cricket Ground by a conjourer, one Roy Hart. A Victory Ball was held in the Village Hall from 8pm to midnight with fancy dress optional and music provided by The Nightswingers (Brighton) Dance Orchestra. It was this ball that was remembered by Pat Ferri who went dressed as a tramp; she said that it was easy for her to play this part because she was not noted for "posh" dressing!

At 10.15pm there was a torchlight procession starting from Sprinks' Stores and a Bonfire and Fireworks display which ended at 11pm. Among the fireworks was The Rainbow Wheel, The Royal Star, The Electric Prince of Wales Feathers (one can only imagine what that was like), and the Huge Golden Palm.

So ended what must have been a memorable and tiring day but a good tribute to those six years of struggle. And for those who heard it, King George V1's speech would have been still ringing in their ears:

"Let us remember those who will not come back: their constancy and courage in battle, their sacrifice and endurance in the face of a merciless enemy; let us remember the men in all the services, and the women in all the services, who have laid down their lives. We have come to the end of our tribulation and they are not with us at the moment of our rejoicing.

Then let us salute in proud gratitude the great host of the living who have brought us to victory. I cannot praise them to the measure of each one's service, for in a total war, the efforts of all rise to the same noble height, and all are devoted to the common purpose.

Armed or unarmed, men and women, you have fought and striven and endured to your utmost. No-one knows that better than I do, and as your King, I thank with a full heart those who bore arms so valiantly on land and sea, or in the air, and all civilians who, shouldering their many burdens, have carried them unflinchingly without complaint

With those memories in our minds, let us think what it was that has upheld us through nearly six years of suffering and peril. The knowledge that everything was at stake: our freedom, our independence, our very existence as a people; but the knowledge also that in defending ourselves we were defending the liberties of the whole world; that our cause was the cause not of this nation only, not of this Empire and Commonwealth only, but of every land where freedom is cherished and law and liberty go hand in hand.

In the darkest hours we knew that the enslaved and isolated peoples of Europe looked to us, their hopes were our hopes, their confidence confirmed our faith. We knew that, if we failed, the last remaining barrier against a worldwide tyranny would have fallen in ruins.

But we did not fail. We kept faith with ourselves and with one another, we kept faith and unity with our great allies. That faith, that unity has carried us to victory through dangers which at times seemed overwhelming."

Cowfold men who had been serving with the Forces were now returning. Jean and Barbara Ross' father came home on 8th May although he was not demobbed until August. Barbara recalls that:

"Mr Farren took us into Horsham to meet him at the station. John, who had only seen photos of his Dad, recognised him as he got off the train and said "That's my Dad"; he was 4 years old. There were flags everywhere."

Pat Sayers remembers her father coming home. She and her mother were in the playing field and a telegram arrived. She remembers her mother opening the telegram and bursting into tears; it told them that her father was coming home. He came into Cowfold by bus and Pat went to meet him. Bunting was put out to welcome him home. Frederick Slocombe, who had been shot down over Germany in 1941 and had been a prisoner of war since that time was released in June and went back to his home in South Wales. He returned to St Peter's School as a teacher in September and eventually became head teacher on Mr Quick's retirement in 1948. Bob Farren's return and demobilisation was delayed:

> *"I was still in this country when the war came to an end in Europe because there was a hold-up in the plans for going overseas. I'm not sure exactly what happened but I and around 70 others trained as air raid architects and the plan was that we would join a force of British heavy bombers to bomb the mainland of Japan. But of course the atom bombs put the lid on that so we were surplus to requirements overnight.*
>
> *I was home on my embarkation leave at the end of August and of course the war in the Far East had literally ended then. I had to go back to the Blackpool "Personnel Disposal Centre". I waited there through October and November, not doing anything really".*

The Japanese surrendered on 15th August after the horrific atomic bomb devastation of Hiroshima and Nagasaki, and formally signed on 2nd September- V-J Day. There appears not to have been any or at least not the same degree of celebration in Cowfold but Colin Rudling, who was in Northumberland with his father and mother, remembers that:

> *"On V-J Day, by which time my father had come back, he wanted to go up to see his parents in Northumberland so we went up there and that day up there they had a carnival; all the trees were lit up with candles in jam jars, and they had bonfires and they made much more of that up there than we did down here. On V-J Day of course a lot of the men had returned so perhaps there was that extra thing to celebrate whereas on V-E Day a lot of them were still over in Europe. The grown-ups may have appreciated it more than we kids did; we didn't think of it as salvation or anything like that".*

Three men did not return home having been killed on active service: Ernest Harvey who at the outbreak of the war was a milkman living at Archers with his mother and father, sister and younger brother; Arthur King; and Alfed Tullett.

* * *

And so this story of Cowfold in WW2 comes to an end. At last after six years the lights came on again.

But the struggle to cope with rationing and food shortages continued long after V-E and V-J Days and after the men returning from the war had begun to settle back into civilian life. Bread and potatoes were rationed for the first time in 1947 and food shortages continued to be exacerbated by the need to help the European countries that had been shattered by the war. The Lend Lease arrangements whereby America loaned equipment and other materiel to Britain to enable it to continue the fight against the Germans meant that British factories had to produce more for export to pay off the debt. Food rationing did not finally come to an end until 4th July 1954 when at midnight restrictions on the sale and purchase of meat and bacon were lifted. This was an incredible fourteen years after rationing was first introduced.

Nevertheless the villagers of Cowfold and the surrounding area had strived to maintain as normal as life as possible in very difficult and sometimes dangerous circumstances, and had prevailed. How proud they must have been of that achievement even if they kept that to themselves and just carried on. There was official recognition of the contribution made by the Home Guard (see above) but in addition the school children received similar commendation for their contribution. In a message sent to every school child in the country, King George wrote:

"Today, as we celebrate victory, I send this personal message to you and all other boys and girls at school. For you have shared in the hardships and dangers of a total war and you have shared no less in the triumph of the Allied Nations.

I know you will always feel proud to belong to a country which was capable of such supreme effort; proud too of parents and elder brothers and sisters who by their courage, endurance and enterprise brought victory. May these qualities be yours as you grow up and join in the common effort to establish among the nations of the world unity and peace.

George RI"

* * *

This story has been built largely around the memories of the 11 people who were children in and around Cowfold during the war. So what was their overall feeling about the experience that they went through over those six years?

Colin Rudling:
"There was a mixture of excitement, some fear but nothing like the adults would have felt, and freedom to do pretty much what we wanted, certainly more so than children are allowed to do today. By the time I became conscious of what was happening around me, the war was the norm; it wasn't as though something dreadful had happened. Life was okay for me, I had my Mum and a nice warm house, enough to eat, and plenty of things to do as well as the routine of going to school where we weren't ill-treated".

Barbara Ross:
"Mum said afterwards that she thought we did not have a very

happy childhood but we just said that we had the total freedom of being out in the country. We were always loved, we were well fed. She was a great disciplinarian; I must have been quite a handful but if Mum said "No" you knew that she meant "No"! That must have been difficult when Dad came home again in the sense of changing roles almost. John could also be a handful in a different way- not naughty but lively.

I wouldn't want my children to go through what we went through. War should not be glorified. We just had to accept the situation because that was what it was and we were part of it. I just think we were lucky to be out in the country. So we didn't have the experiences of people who lived in London or in cities like Coventry. I think growing up in a village is the best thing that could happen to you. I think it is a lovely life and I don't regret any of that. You knew everybody and everybody knew you".

Jean Ross:

"In some ways I grew up mentally more than I think I would have done otherwise because Mum would talk to me as I was that bit older than Barbara, especially towards the end of the war. Cowfold was only about a third of the size it is now so you did know everyone and there was a strong sense of community".

Mary Matthews:

"Life went on as normally as possible. I can't remember being terrified at any time because I think parents tried their best to shield children from the awful things that were happening. As farmers we had to make sure that everything carried on as normal. But I think I possibly was frightened at night time when we used to hear the bombers going over because we never knew where the bombs would be dropped".

Pat Ferri:
"I was 10 when war started and 16 when it finished and I had accepted everything that went on. With age you see things differently and things were done then that make you wonder why. You can be critical in a way that you cannot as a child".

At least two main themes underpin this story which may have lessons for us all. The first is the resilience and adaptability, and not least the courage, that humans are capable of displaying when faced with an extreme situation such as war and the threat of invasion. Time and again this adaptability and the sheer ability to try to maintain as normal a life in abnormal times as possible, shines through the experiences you have read about in this book. This should give us all hope!

The second is the ability for a community to come together when in peril and to be melded by a common purpose. Cowfold villagers were a strong community in WW2 and although there were social hierarchies, everyone appears to have wanted to pitch in and help whenever possible. What does this tell us about the way that communities have evolved today? And does it take a situation like a war or the threat of war to bring out the best in us?

I would like to think that faced with the situation experienced by the villagers during the six years of WW2, we would respond in a similar way. But the obvious hope is that we would not have to face this and that the lights will remain switched on.

Acknowledgements

This book could not have been written was it not for the willingness of the eleven people who were children during the war to share their experiences and memories. I am deeply grateful to them for their patience, kindness and hospitality during nearly 24 hours of interviews. This is as much their story as that of their parents and grandparents and the other villagers of Cowfold and the surrounding area.

In setting these memories within the context of the momentous events of the six years of war, I have made extensive use of the internet including Wikipedia for background information; this is an amazing source of information and knowledge and is one of the positives of having this facility. I am very grateful to all those who are involved in ensuring that the facts are available.

Mike Gething has contributed a significant piece of research on the airfields and Allied squadrons that operated around Cowfold – see Appendix C – for which I am very grateful. I have also drawn on the following sources of information all of which have been immensely helpful in constructing what happened during that period and for which I am also very grateful: Elizabeth Arthur (nee

Chase)'s recollections in her booklet *Recollections of Shermanbury…
and more*; Stewart Angell's account of the Home Guard Auxiliary
Units in *Secret Sussex Resistance*; the St Peter's School log book and
Admissions Register which the Head Teacher Giles Kolter kindly
made available to me; *D-Day West Sussex* by Ian Greig, Kim Leslie and
Alan Redman; *When the Whistle Blew* – the story of West Grinstead,
Partridge Green and Dial Post by the West Grinstead Local History
Group; *Horsham – a history* by Susan Haines; *West Sussex under
attack* by Chris Butler; PC Albert Elliott's scrap books of cuttings
and jottings covering the WW2 period kindly made available by his
daughter June West; a large range of war-time memorabilia, leaflets
and advertisements that are part of the Bob Farren archive; articles
that have appeared in the BBC History magazine; "*A Green and
Pleasant Land*" by Ursula Buchan; "*When the children came home*"
by Julie Summers; DVD and other film material including *Wartime
Farm* a BBC production by Acorn Media UK.

Appendix A

The 1939 England and Wales Register

The data for the Register was collected on 29th September 1939 and records people who were in a particular home at the time of recording.

Its initial purpose was to produce National Identity Cards, but the Register later came to be multi-functional, first as an aid in the use of ration books and later helping officials record the movement of the civilian population over the following decades; from 1948 it formed the basis for the National Health Service Register. The 1939 Register is therefore an extremely important genealogical resource for the rich detail and information recorded for each person and household.

The Register includes extra information, such as whether an individual had volunteered as an air raid warden or was a special constable. Some records have been redacted to protect the privacy of those still alive at the time of redaction so unfortunately there are gaps in the names listed below for people living in and around Cowfold on 29th September 1939, and in the houses they lived in; however 1,138 names are recorded. The surnames shown for women are, for married women, the surname of their husband, and for single women their maiden name. The Cowfold residents are listed below by surname, place of residence and occupation.

The breakdown by occupation (and excluding 47 lay brothers and monks at St Hugh's Monastery) is as follows: 11% were involved in agriculture of various types, 20% provided services to the community (for example maids, domestic services, gardeners, chauffeurs), 4% were craftsmen, 4% were in retail, 5% were professionals of various types, 2% lived by private means and 4% were either retired or incapacitated in some way.

10% of the residents were school children and 2% were under school age (under 5 years old).

"Domestic duties" shown as an occupation denotes a housewife, relative or other female occupant looking after a home or undertaking various duties in the home or working elsewhere as a domestic. These residents made up 38% of the community, by far the largest sector.

Between 2nd and 4th September 1939 nearly 300 evacuees arrived in Cowfold, including 97 children and 9 teachers from Christchurch Parish School, Croydon, and were billeted in and around the village. With a few exceptions, the Register does not record an evacuee but where in a household there is a mother and/or child with a different surname, the likelihood is that that person was an evacuee and that is shown below.

Name	Occupation	Residence	Comment
Ackerley Albert Mr	Cowman	Trenchmore Cottage	
Ackerley Ellen Mrs	Domestic duties	Trenchmore Cottage	
Akehurst Alfred Mr	Builders General Labourer	2 Council Cottages	
Akehurst Kergyia Mrs	Domestic duties	2 Council Cottages	
Akehurst Henry Mr	Estate Foreman	Hill Farm Cottages	
Akehurst Henrietta Mrs	Domestic duties	Hill Farm Cottages	
Aland Stephen Mr	Grocer's Clerk	Oakfield	
Aland H M Mrs	Domestic duties	Oakfield	
Allchin Nicola Mrs	Domestic duties	Cowfold Lodge	Evacuee
Allchin William	At school	Cowfold Lodge	Evacuee
Allen Stephen Mr	Insurance Agent	Ellerslie	
Allen Ellen Mrs	Domestic duties	Ellerslie	
Ankerson James Mr	Farmer and Butcher	High Hurst Farm	
Ankerson May Mrs	Domestic duties	High Hurst Farm	
Ankerson Valentine Miss	Butcher's Cashier	High Hurst Farm	
Ankerson Lily Miss	Butcher's Cashier	High Hurst Farm	
Ankerson Joan Miss	Domestic duties	High Hurst Farm	
Ankerson Thea Miss	Dairy work/ Assistant Cashier	High Hurst Farm	
Annatt Elizabeth Mrs (widow)	Retired	Wood Grange	
Anscombe Thomas Mr	Farm Labourer	New Steyne House	
Anscombe Frances Miss	Domestic duties	New Steyne House	
Anscombe Sarah Miss	Domestic duties	New Steyne House	
Archard Kathleen Miss	Schoolteacher	Carleon	
Arnold Henry Mr (widower)	Pensioner	South Lodge Stables, Lwr Beeding	
Arnold Helena Miss	Domestic duties	South Lodge Stables, Lwr Beeding	
Ashby Alice Mrs	Domestic duties	Lydford Farm	Evacuee
Ashman Marie Mrs	Domestic duties	Cottlands	Evacuee
Ashman Frances	Under school age (2 years)	Cottlands	Evacuee
Atkins Ethel Miss	Domestic duties	Gratwick Farm	

Name	Occupation	Residence	Comment
Austin Kathleen Mrs	Domestic duties	4 Woodville Terrace	
Bacon George Mr	Coal Hoist Labourer	2 Glenthorne	
Bacon Mabel Mrs	Domestic duties	2 Glenthorne	
Bacon Annie Mrs	Domestic duties	2 Glenthorne	
Bacon Mary	Under school age (3 years)	2 Glenthorne	
Baggett Elsie Mrs	Domestic duties	Stable Cottage, Clock Hse	Evacuee
Baggett Jeanette	Under school age	Stable Cottage, Clock Hse	Evacuee
Baillie Dennis Mr	Shop Assistant	Allfreys (Garage)	
Banfield Helen Miss	Maid	Brookhill House	
Barham Lilly Miss	Nursery Probationer	Woldringfold	
Barlow Frederick Mr	Garden Labourer	Gratwick Lodge	
Barlow Agnes Mrs	Domestic duties	Gratwick Lodge	
Barnard Edward Mr	Railway Signalman (retired)	3 Elm Grove	
Barnett William Mr	Cowman	Little Patches	
Barnett Catherine Mrs	Domestic duties	Little Patches	
Barnett Winifred Mrs	Domestic duties	Little Patches	
Barnett Bernard	At school	Little Patches	
Barrow Cicely Miss	Staff Nurse (Resident Home)	South Lodge, Lwr Beeding	
Barton Alice Miss	Domestic Servant	South Leas	
Barton George Mr	Grocer's Warehouse-man (ret'd)	2 Huntscroft Gardens	
Barton Mary Mrs	Domestic duties	2 Huntscroft Gardens	
Bassett William Mr	Builder's Labourer	6 Council Cottages	
Bassett Mary Mrs	Domestic duties	6 Council Cottages	
Bayliss John Mr	General Labourer	The Wish	Special Constable
Bayliss Catherine Mrs	Domestic duties	The Wish	
Baxter Florence Miss	District Nurse/ Midwife	5 Church Terrace	

Name	Occupation	Residence	Comment
Beale Clive Mr	Research Engineer	Allfreys	
Beale Evelyn Mrs	Domestic duties	Allfreys	
Beale Alison	At school	Allfreys	
Bean Edith Miss	Domestic duties	Rossmore, Parkminster	
Bean Ethel Miss	Domestic duties	Rossmore, Parkminster	
Beavis Eliza Mrs (widow)	Domestic duties	2 Mill Lane, Lwr Beeding	
Belton Charles Mr	Blacksmith	3 Oakfield Cottages	
Belton Gertrude Mrs	Domestic duties	3 Oakfield Cottages	
Belton Leslie	At school	3 Oakfield Cottages	
Belton Doris Miss	Cook	Allfreys	
Belton Sarah Miss	Domestic worker	Thornden	
Bennett Albert Mr	Chauffeur	The Cottage, Clock house	
Bennett Eileen Miss	Nursery Maid	Allfreys	
Benson Daisy Miss	Saleswoman Drapery	Wythe	Evacuee
Bidwell William Mr	Gardener (retired)	Cotlands Cottages	
Bidwell Frances Mrs	Domestic duties	Cotlands Cottages	
Blaber Albert Mr	Chauffeur	Brookhill Cottage	
Blaber Beatrice Mrs	Domestic duties	Brookhill Cottage	
Black Stephen Mr	Journalist	Gorsedean, Mill Lane	
Black Joyce Mrs	Domestic duties	Gorsedean, Mill Lane	
Blackman Herbert Mr	Farm Carter/ Cowman	Wallhurst Manor	
Blake Jack Mr	Horseman	2 Smiths Cross Cottage	
Blake Walter Mr	Cowman	Lydford Farm	
Blake Edith Mrs	Domestic duties	Lydford Farm	
Blatch Robert Mr	Baker's Assistant	1 Huntscroft Gardens	
Bottomley Claude Mr	Gamekeeper	14 Mount Pleasant	
Bonfield Helen Miss	Maid	Brookhill House	

Name	Occupation	Residence	Comment
Boniface Dorothy Miss	Domestic service	Oakendene	
Boutereau Andre Mr	Secretary Companion	Cowfold Lodge	
Boxall Albert Mr	Gardener	Carleon	
Boxall Lilian Mrs	Domestic duties	Carleon	
Boxall Reginald Mr	Bricklayer	Carleon	
Boxall Albert Mr	Carpenter	Holmstead	
Boxall Hilda Mrs	Domestic duties	Holmstead	
Boxall Peter	At school	Holmstead	
Boyles Robert Mr	Garden boy	Drewitts Lodge	
Braithwaite Albert	At school	Stonefield Cottages	Evacuee
Braithwaite Mary	At school	7 Council Cottages	Evacuee
Breckinridge John Mr	Independent	Cowfold Lodge	
Bringloe Charles Mr	Groom/Poultryman	1 Oakendene New Cottages	
Bringloe Kathleen Mrs	Domestic duties	1 Oakendene New Cottages	
Bristow Clara Miss	Private Nurse	Drewitts	
Brooker Charlie Mr	Farm Labourer	Frithlands	
Brooker Clara Mrs	Domestic duties	Frithlands	
Brooker Harry Mr	Farm Labourer	Gratwick Cottages	
Brooker Fanny Mrs	Domestic duties	Gratwick Cottages	
Brooker Arthur Mr	Cowman	Gratwick Cottages	
Brooker Elsie Miss	Kitchen Maid	Gratwick Cottages	
Brown Gladys Mrs	Domestic duties	Allfreys Cottages	Evacuee
Brown Howard	Under school age (2 years)	Allfreys Cottages	Evacuee
Browning Ada Miss	Elementary School Teacher	Fairhill	Evacuee
Bullock T Mrs (widow)	Housework	Oakfield	
Bunce Alan	Under school age (3 years)	Little Brook	Evacuee

Name	Occupation	Residence	Comment
Burchall Stanley Mr	Chauffeur	Ivorys	
Burdock Frank Mr	Butcher's Assistant	Bulls Bridge	
Burley Harry Mr	Gardener	Westland Cottage	
Burley Violet Mrs	Domestic duties	Westland Cottage	
Burley Edward Mr	Under Gardener	Westland Cottage	
Butcher Harry Mr	Boot Repairer	5 Elm Grove	
Butcher Alice Mrs	Domestic duties	5 Elm Grove	
Button Florence Miss	Retired	The Red Lion	
Buxton Gordon Mr	Chauffeur	Stonefield Cottages	
Buxton Mary Mrs	Domestic duties	Stonefield Cottages	
Buxton Phyllis	Domestic duties	Stonefield Cottages	
Buxton Olive Mrs	Domestic (visitor)	Olde House	Evacuee
Buxton Gordon	At school	Olde House	Evacuee
Caffyn George Mr	Gardener	Little Brook	
Caffyn Sylvia Mrs	Domestic duties	Little Brook	
Campbell Gwendoline	At school	Brook Farm	Evacuee
Campbell Joan	At school	Hazlebank	Evacuee
Capsey Benjamin Mr	Farmer	North Farm	
Capsey Mona Mrs	Domestic duties	North Farm	
Capsey Richard	At school	North Farm	
Card Royston Mr	Grocer Chargehand	Godshill Farm	
Card Marjorie Miss	Kitchenmaid	Godshill Farm	
Carter Derek	At school	2 Oakfield Cottages	Evacuee
Carter Elizabeth Mrs	Domestic duties	Little Brook	Evacuee
Carter Gwendoline	At school	Oakendene Gdner's Cott	Evacuee
Carter Harold Mr	Chauffeur	Ivorys Cottage	
Carter Ellen Mrs	Domestic duties	Ivorys Cottage	
Carter Jane Mrs	Domestic duties	Ivorys Cottage	
Carter Margery	Under school age (4 years)	Ivorys Cottage	

Name	Occupation	Residence	Comment
Carter Herbert Mr	Chauffeur	Eastridge Lodge	
Carter Margaret Mrs	Domestic duties	Eastridge Lodge	
Carter John Mr	Stockman/Farm Labourer	Homefields	
Carter Mary Mrs	Domestic duties	Homefields	
Carthusian monks	47 plus lay brothers	St Hugh's Monastery	
Carver Henry Mr	Farm Stockman	Bulls Bridge	
Chappell Edward	At school	Fair View	Evacuee
Charman Frederick Mr	Lorry Driver	Archers	
Charman Vera Mrs	Domestic duties	Archers	
Cheriman William Mr	Gardener	Longhouse (Stables)	
Cheriman Caroline Mrs	Domestic duties	Longhouse (Stables)	
Childs Emma Mrs	Domestic duties	Sadlers	Evacuee
Chipchase Ethel Miss	Domestic worker	Thornden	
Chipchase Florence Miss	Lady's Maid	South Lodge, Lwr Beeding	
Chowne Edward Mr	Farm Carter	Oakendene Farm	
Chowne Alice Mrs	Domestic duties	Oakendene Farm	
Chowne Doris Miss	Dairy Girl	Oakendene Farm	
Christie Rose Mrs (widow)	Household and Farm work	Eastlands	
Clark Andrew Mr	Farm Carter	St Michaels	
Clarner (?) Dorothy Miss	Housemaid	Brook Farm	
Coates Violet Mrs	Domestic duties	Wallhurst Lodge	
Collier Irene	At school	Hill House Farm	Evacuee
Collier Maureen	At school	Hill House Farm	Evacuee
Colvin Hester Mrs	Private means	Woldringfold	
Constable George Mr	Gardener	Marlow	
Constable Edith Mrs	Domestic duties	Marlow	

Name	Occupation	Residence	Comment
Constable Olivia Miss	Private means	Clock House	
Cook Olive Mrs	Housewife	1 Oakfield Cottages	Evacuee
Coquerelle Agnes Miss	Domestic worker	Thornden	
Coquerelle Julien Mr	Compositor	Little Parkminster	
Coquerelle Kathleen Mrs	Domestic duties	Little Parkminster	
Coquerelle Raymond Mr	Carpenter Apprentice	Little Parkminster	
Court Philip	At school	Parkminster	Evacuee
Court Sylvia	At school	Little Parkminster	Evacuee
Cordell Joan Miss	School Teacher	The Vicarage	Evacuee
Cox Herbert Mr	Engineer/Captain RN (retired)	Denwood	
Cox Alice Mrs	Domestic duties	Denwood	
Cox John Mr	General Labourer	The Ferns, Mill Lane, Lwr Beeding	
Cox Mary Mrs	Domestic duties	The Ferns, Mill Lane, Lwr Beeding	
Cox Pamela	At school	Old Woldringfold	Evacuee
Cox Richard	At school	Stonefield Cottages	Evacuee
Cox Samuel Mr	Cowman	Gratwick Cottages	
Craven Eric Mr	Chauffeur	Woldringfold (Stables)	
Craven Emily Mrs	Domestic duties	Woldringfold (Stables)	
Crossfield John Mr	Poultry Dealer	Frithlands	
Crossfield Caroline Mrs	Domestic duties	Frithlands	
Crossfield Oliver Mr	Motor Driver	Frithlands	
Cubitt Rosamund Mrs	Domestic duties	Thornden	
Cummins Josephine Mrs	Domestic duties	Goodyears Farm, Mill Lane	
Curry Grace	Not at school (ill)	Noah's Ark Café	Evacuee
Dale Arthur Mr	Greenhouse Gardener	2 Mill Lane, Lwr Beeding	
Dale Elizabeth Mrs	Domestic duties	2 Mill Lane, Lwr Beeding	

Name	Occupation	Residence	Comment
Dale Margaret Miss	Domestic duties	Gorsedean, Mill Lane, Lwr Beeding	
Dalley Mary Mrs	Domestic duties	Woodville	
Das Correia Dores Miss	Domestic Maid	Ivorys	
Davey Job Mr	Council Labourer	Brick Kiln Cottages, Lwr Beeding	
Davidson Mary Mrs (widow)	Retired	The Red Lion	
Davies Kathleen Miss	Parlourmaid	Hill House Farm	
Davies Mabel Mrs	Housewife	St Michaels	
Dedman Alfred Mr	Huntsman	32 New Cottages, Lwr Beeding	
Dedman Dora Mrs	Domestic duties	32 New Cottages, Lwr Beeding	
Deforges William Mr	Pensioner	5 Margaret Cottages	
Deforges Elizabeth Mrs	Charing	5 Margaret Cottages	
De Jesus Maria Miss	Domestic Maid	Ivorys	
Demmett Gerald Mr	Chauffeur	Old Woldringfold	
Demmett Dorothy Mrs	Domestic duties	Old Woldringfold	
Denman Arthur Mr	Head Gardener	6 Mill Lane, Lwr Beeding	
Denman Emily Mrs	Domestic duties	6 Mill Lane, Lwr Beeding	
Denman Gladys Miss	Gardener	6 Mill Lane, Lwr Beeding	
Denton Doris Mrs	Waitress	Eastridge	
Denyer Agnes Miss	Incapacitated	Woldringfold	
Dewar Letitia Lady (widow)	Private means	Brookhill House	
Dickins Beatrice Miss	Dispenser/Book-keeper	Furzefield House	VAD and Gas Officer
Dickins Sidney Dr	Physician/Surgeon	Furzefield House	
Dixon Arthur Mr	Butcher	Palmeston House	
Dixon Maud Mrs	Domestic duties	Palmeston House	
Dixon Norma	At school	Bunton	Evacuee
Donne George Mr	Solicitor	Lydford	
Donne Henrietta Mrs	Domestic duties	Lydford	

Name	Occupation	Residence	Comment
Douglas Millicent Mrs	Domestic duties	Maryland Farm	Evacuee
Doyle Peter Mr	Farm Labourer	Westlands Cottage	
Doyle Lily Mrs	Domestic duties	Westlands Cottage	
Doyle John	At school	Westlands Cottage	
Draycott Dorothy Miss	Housemaid	Woldringfold	
Dudeney Jean Miss	Cook	The Red House	
Dutton Catherine Miss	Cook	Clock House	
Dymond Kathleen Miss	Maid	Cowfold Lodge	
Eade Thomas Mr	Carpenter	Oaklea	
Eade Bertha Mrs	Domestic duties	Oaklea	
Ede William Mr	Hotel Odd Man	Church Terrace	
Ede Elizabeth Mrs	Dressmaker	Church Terrace	
Edwards Alfred Mr	House Painter/ Decorator	Ingleside	
Edwards Winifred Mrs	Domestic duties	Ingleside	
Edwards Irene Miss	Hairdresser	Ingleside	
Eggleton William Mr	Gamekeeper	Hooklands	
Eggleton Dorothy Mrs	Domestic duties	Hooklands	
Elliott Albert PC	Police Constable	Police House	
Elliott Lilian Mrs	Domestic duties	Police House	
Elliott June	At school	Police House	
Elliott David	Under school age (3 years)	Police House	
Elliott-Cooper Sir R	Civil Engineer	Clock House	
Elliott-Cooper Fanny Lady	Domestic duties	Clock House	
Englefield Frances Miss	Children's Nurse	Allfreys	
Etherton Charles Mr	Church Clerk and Verger	8 Huntscroft Gardens	
Etherton Ethel Mrs	Domestic duties	8 Huntscroft Gardens	
Evans Agnes Mrs	Domestic duties	Stable Cttge,Clockhouse	Evacuee
Evans David	Under school age (1 year)	StableCttge, Clock House	Evacuee

Name	Occupation	Residence	Comment
Faires Harry Mr	Farm Labourer	Parkgate, Lwr Beeding	
Faires Sarah Mrs	Domestic duties	Parkgate, Lwr Beeding	
Faires Warwick Mr	Horticultural Worker	Parkgate, Lwr Beeding	
Faires Jack Mr	Lorry Driver	Fairhill	
Faires Gladys Mrs	Domestic duties	Fairhill	
Faires Kathleen Miss	Parlour maid	Brookhill House	
Farr Alan Mr	Estate Laundry	The Laundry, Woldringford	
Farr Eva Mrs	Domestic duties	The Laundry, Woldringfold	
Farren James Mr	Blacksmith/Motor Engineer	White Lined House	
Farren Olive Mrs	Domestic duties	White Lined House	
Farren Frederick Mr	Motor and Electrical Engineer	Sussex House	
Farren Dorothy Mrs	Domestic duties	Sussex House	
Farren Robert	At school	Sussex House	
Farren Dorothy	At school	Sussex House	
Foard George Mr	Dairy farmer	Kings Farm	
Foard Elizabeth Mrs	Domestic duties	Kings Farm	
Foley Mildred Miss	Store Keeper, Red Cross	South Lodge, Lwr Beeding	
Ford Amy Mrs	Unpaid domestic worker	Thornden	Evacuee
Ford Audrey	At school	Thornden	Evacuee
Ford Edward Mr	Head Gardener	Oakendene Gardener's Cottage	
Ford Edith Mrs	Domestic duties	Oakendene Gardener's Cottage	
Forstner Theresa Miss	Cook	Cowfold Lodge	
Foster Gertrude Mrs (widow)	Domestic duties	3 Drewitts Cottages	
Fowler Cuthbert Mr Observer Corps	Builder	The Brown House	
Fowler Joyce Mrs	Domestic duties	The Brown House	
Fowler Florence Mrs	Domestic duties	3 Council Cottages	

Name	Occupation	Residence	Comment
Fowler Florence Mrs (widow)	Domestic duties	Oakcroft	
Fowler Frederick Mr	Builder/Contractor	Huntscroft	
Fowler Louisa Mrs	Domestic duties	Huntscroft	
Fowler Ethel Miss	Private means	Huntscroft	Red Cross
Fowler Stephen Mr	Building Contractor	South Leas	Observer Corps
Fowler Olive Mrs	Domestic duties	South Leas	Billeting Officer
Francis Dorothy Miss	Lady's Maid	Brook Farm	
Francis John Mr	Retired	3 Woodville Terrace	
Francis Ellen Mrs	Domestic duties	3 Woodville Terrace	
Freed Milly Mrs	Domestic duties	Rosslyn	
Freed Joyce Miss	Window Dresser	Rosslyn	
Freeman Walter Mr	Retired	2 Margaret Cottages	
Freeman Rose Mrs	Housewife	2 Margaret Cottages	
Fretter Charles Mr	Butler	"Fretridge", Brook Hill	
Fretter Bettie Mrs	Domestic duties	"Fretridge", Brook Hill	
Fry Clara Mrs	Domestic duties	Westleigh	
Fry Mary Mrs (widow)	Domestic duties	Church Lodge	
Gander Charles Mr	Farmer	Frithknowle	
Gander Adelaide Mrs	Domestic duties	Frithknowle	
Gander Daisy Mrs	Domestic duties	Thornden (Garage)	
Gander Ernest Mr	Farm Labourer	Brick Kiln Cottages, Lwr Beeding	
Gander Sarah Mrs	Domestic duties	Brick Kiln Cottages, Lwr Beeding	
Gander Ronald Mr	Dairy Farmer	Capons Farm	
Gander Winifred Mrs	Domestic duties	Capons Farm	
Gander Anthony	At school	Capons Farm	
Gannell Edward Mr	Dairyman	Wilcox Cottage	
Gannell Katy Mrs	Domestic duties	Wilcox Cottage	
Gannell John	At school	Wilcox Cottage	
Gardener Harold Mr	Chauffeur	5 Huntscroft Gardens	
Gardener Edna Mrs	Domestic duties	5 Huntscroft Gardens	

Name	Occupation	Residence	Comment
Gardner Charles Mr	Private means	Barnfield	
Gates Thomas Mr	Builder's Clerk (retired)	[No house recorded]	
Gates Rose Mrs	Domestic duties	[No house recorded]	
Gaurdrey Beatrice Mrs	Domestic duties	Capons Farm	Evacuee
George Emily Mrs	Domestic duties	4 Elm Grove	Evacuee
George Elizabeth	At school	4 Elm Grove	Evacuee
Gibbs Gordon Mr	Farm Bailiff	Brook Farm Cottages	
Gibbs Edna Mrs	Domestic duties	Brook Farm Cottages	
Gibbs Merrick	At school	Brook Farm Cottages	
Gilbert Charles Mr	Milk Roundsman	South Lodge Cottage, Lwr Beeding	
Gilbert Edith Mrs	Domestic duties	South Lodge Cottage, Lwr Beeding	
Gilson Sofia Miss	Café Proprietor	Noah's Ark Café	
Gilson Harriet Mrs (widow)	Domestic duties	Noah's Ark Cafe	
Gittins Margaret Mrs	Domestic duties	Barnfield Garage	
Goacher James Mr	Butcher	Olde House	Special constable
Goacher Margaret Mrs	Domestic duties	Olde House	
Goacher Joyce	At school	Olde House	
Goddard Thomas Mr	Cowman	Hill Farm Cottages	
Goddard Florence Mrs	Domestic duties	Hill Farm Cottages	
Godman Alice Dame	Commandant Red Cross	South Lodge, Lwr Beeding	
Godman Edith Miss	Nursing Auxiliary Service	South Lodge, Lwr Beeding	
Godman Eva Miss	Nursing Auxiliary Service	South Lodge, Lwr Beeding	
Godman Sir Charles	Private means	Woldringfold	
Godman Lady Olive	Domestic duties	Woldringfold	
Goff Kathleen Miss	Domestic servant	North Farm	
Goncalves Maria Miss	Domestic Maid	Ivorys	
Golding Winifred Mrs	Domestic duties	2 South Lodge Cottage, Lwr Beeding	

Name	Occupation	Residence	Comment
Golds Thomas Mr	General Builder's Labourer	Cottlands Cottages	
Golds Mary Mrs	Domestic duties	Cottlands Cottages	
Golds Thomas Mr	Under Cowman	Cottlands Cottages	
Gordon-Smith Sir Alan	Managing Director	Wallhurst Manor	Deputy Lieutenant
Gordon-Smith Lady Hilda	Domestic duties	Wallhurst Manor	
Gordon-Smith Kathleen	Domestic duties	Wallhurst Manor	
Gosling Marjorie Miss	Housemaid	Brookhill House	
Goulburn Arthur Mr	Retired	Kings Barn	
Grainger Frances Mr	Farm Labourer	Crateman's Farm	
Grainger Gertrude Mrs	Domestic duties	Crateman's Farm	
Grainger William Mr	Gamekeeper	Wilcox Cottage	
Grainger Rosa Mrs	Domestic duties	Wilcox Cottage	
Grainger Lewis Mr	Farm Labourer	Wilcox Cottage	
Gray Sidney Mr	Cowman	The Bungalow, Brook Farm	
Gray Ethel Mrs	Domestic duties	The Bungalow, Brook Farm	
Gray Keith Mr	Apprenticed Motor Mechanic	The Bungalow, Brook Farm	
Greenslade William Mr	Farmer	Lodge Farm, Woldringfold	
Gregory Alice Mrs	Domestic duties	Hill Farm Cottages	
Gregory Edith Mrs	Domestic duties	Hill Farm Cottages	
Gregory Henry Mr	Builder's Labourer	1 Woodville Terrace	
Gregory May Mrs	Domestic duties	1 Woodville Terrace	
Grinchard Albert Mr	Cowman	Trenchmore Cottage	
Grinchard Ellen Mrs	Domestic duties	Trenchmore Cottage	
Grindley Jessie Miss	Housemaid	South Lodge, Lwr Beeding	
Haggerstone William Mr	Motor Mechanic	Cottlands Platts	
Hains Amy Mrs	Housewife	Wood Grange	
Hale George Mr	House Decorator	3 Huntscroft Gardens	
Hall Henrietta Miss	Nurse	Clock House	

Name	Occupation	Residence	Comment
Halloran Doris Miss	Senior Staff Nurse	South Lodge, Lwr Beeding	
Hamburger Siegfried Mr	Butler	Barnfield	
Hamburger Angela Mrs	Cook	Barnfield	
Hanley Mary Miss	Evacuee Helper	Hill Farm House	
Harland Edith Mrs (widow)	Domestic duties	Crateman's Farm	
Harris George Mr	Farm Labourer	Frithknowle	
Harris Joan	At school	Brookhill House	Evacuee
Harrison Amy Mrs (widow)	Laundress	Mill Lane, Lwr Beeding	
Harrison Alfred Mr	Gardener	Mill Lane, Lwr Beeding	
Harrison Elizabeth Miss	Domestic duties	Mill Lane, Lwr Beeding	
Harrison Gladys Mrs	Domestic duties	Rosslyn	
Harrod Stanley Mr	Dairyman	11 Hillside, Lwr Beeding	
Harvey Ernest Mr	Farm Labourer	Archers	
Harvey Elizabeth Mrs	Domestic duties	Archers	
Harvey Ernest Mr	Milkman	Archers	
Harvey Elsie Miss	Domestic	Archers	
Harvey John	At school	Archers	
Haskins James Mr	Labourer	Banfield Cottages	
Haskins Minnie Mrs	Domestic duties	Banfield Cottages	
Hawkins Henry Mr	Farmer	Chates	
Hawkins Winifred Mrs	Domestic duties	Chates	
Hawkins Josie	Under school age (1 month)	Chates	
Hayes Doreen	At school	Tremosa	Evacuee
Haynes Ivy Mrs	Domestic duties	Brook Farm	
Haystaff William Mr	Head Gardener	Barnfield Lodge	
Haystaff Irene Mrs	Domestic duties	Barnfield Lodge	
Haystaff Denise	At school	Barnfield Lodge	
Heasman Walter Mr	Gardener	Wallhurst Lodge	
Heasman Eliza Mrs	Domestic duties	Wallhurst Lodge	

Name	Occupation	Residence	Comment
Heath Edward Mr	Metal Worker/ Plater	Wood Grange	
Hedger Herbert Mr	Farm Carter	Potters Green	
Hedger Dorothy Mrs	Domestic duties	Potters Green	
Hedger Edward Mr	Gardener	Potters Green	
Hedger Raymond	At school	Potters Green	
Henley Horace Mr	Farm Foreman	Clock House Farm	
Henley Vera Mrs	Domestic duties	Clock House Farm	
Henley Horace Mr	Rabbit Trapper	Clock House Farm	
Hermon Nellie Miss	Private means	Clock House	WVS
Herridan Edward	At school	4 Drewitts Cottages	Evacuee
Hill Emily Miss	Domestic duties	South View, Mill Lane, Lwr Beeding	
Hillman Frank Mr	Council Roadman	Church Gate	
Hills Edward Mr	Cowman	Potters House	
Hills Annie Mrs	Domestic duties	Potters House	
Hills Albert	At school	Potters House	
Hills John	At school	Potters House	
Hills Royston	At school	Potters House	
Hills Richard Mr	Gardener	Lydford	
Hills Blanche Mrs	Domestic duties	Lydford	
Hills William Mr	Gardener	The Gables	
Hills Humphripa (?) Mrs	Domestic duties	The Gables	
Hills Dot Miss	Builder's Shorthand Typist	The Gables	WVS
Hitchcock Leonard Mr	Chauffeur	Wallhurst Manor Cottage	
Hitchcock Marianne Mrs	Domestic duties	Wallhurst Manor Cottage	
Hoad Dorothy Mrs	Domestic duties	Brook Farm	Evacuee
Hoad Bryan	Under school age (2 years)	Brook Farm	Evacuee
Hobden Archibald Mr	Cowman/Carter	West Ridge Farm	
Hobson Elizabeth Miss	Private means	Furzefield House	
Hodgson Arthur Mr	Private means	Brook Farm	
Hodgson Constance Mrs	Domestic duties	Brook Farm	

Name	Occupation	Residence	Comment
Hodgson Edward Mr	Private means	Barnfield	
Hodgson Anna Mrs	Domestic duties	Barnfield	
Hodgson Barbara Miss	Private means	Barnfield	
Hodgson Emily Miss	Domestic servant	Wallhurst Manor	
Hogsflesh Bessie Miss	Paid Domestic	Clock House	
Holden John Mr	Wheelwright	4 Oakfield Cottages	
Holden Abigail Mrs	Domestic duties	4 Oakfield Cottages	
Holden Leslie Mr	Farm Lorry Driver	5 Council Cottages	
Holden Florence Mrs	Domestic duties	5 Council Cottages	
Holden Royston	Under school age (3 months)	5 Council Cottages	
Holden William	Under school age (4 years)	5 Council Cottages	
Holden Mary Mrs (widow)	Domestic duties	4 Mill Lane, Lwr Beeding	
Holland Annie Mrs	Domestic duties	Little Brook	
Holland Doris Miss	Dressmaker	Little Brook	
Holland John	At school	Little Brook	
Hood Henry Mr	Stockman	Taintfield Cottages	
Hood Edith Mrs	School Caretaker	Taintfield Cottages	
Hood Cecil	At school	Taintfield Cottages	
Hoper Dorothea Miss	Private means	Hill House Farm	
Hoper Edith Miss	Private means	Hill House Farm	
Hoper Emma Miss	Private means	Hill House Farm	
Hoper Mary Miss	Private means	Hill House Farm	
Hornung Charles Mr	Director British Sugar	Ivorys	
Hornung Olive Mrs	Domestic duties	Ivorys	
Hornung Aileen Miss	Domestic duties	Ivorys	
Hother Albert Mr	Kitchen Gardener	3 Mill Lane, Lwr Beeding	
Hother Caroline Mrs	Domestic duties	3 Mill Lane, Lwr Beeding	
Howard Albert Mr	Gardener	Kings Barn	
Howard Mary Mrs	Domestic duties	Kings Barn	
Howard Ethel Mrs (widow)	President WI	Brownings	
Howard James Mr	Council Roadman	Oakleigh	

Name	Occupation	Residence	Comment
Howard John Mr	Dairy and Stock Farmer	Eastlands	
Howard Christine Miss	Household and Farm work	Eastlands	
Howett Ellen Mrs (widow)	Domestic duties	Lodge Farm, Woldringfold	
Hudnott Charles Mr	Chef	Ivorys	
Hudson Alice Miss	Domestic duties	Huntscroft	
Huggett Joan	At school	Brookhill House	Evacuee
Hughes George Mr	Painter/Decorator	Glen Lyn	
Hughes Daisy Mrs	Domestic duties	Glen Lyn	
Hulbert Betty	At school	14 Mount Pleasant	Evacuee
Hulbert Marjorie	At school	14 Mount Pleasant	Evacuee
Humphrey Edgar Mr	Sub-postmaster/Shopkeeper	The Post Office	
Humphrey Edith Mrs	Domestic duties	The Post Office	
Humphrey Bessie Miss	P.O. Assistant	The Post Office	
Humphrey Edith Miss	Domestic duties	The Post Office	
Humphrey Lucy Mrs (widow)	Domestic duties	Arundale	
Humphrey Daisy Miss	Teacher	Arundale	
Humphrey May Miss	Draper and Confectioner	Arundale	
Hunnisett Philip Mr	Chauffeur	2 Drewitts Cottages	
Hunnisett Ada Mrs	Domestic duties	2 Drewitts Cottages	
Ireland William Mr	Sadler/Harness Maker	Sadlers	
Ireland Charlotte Mrs (widow)	Domestic duties	Sadlers	
Ireland Marjorie Miss	Draper's Assistant	Sadlers	
Isted Lily Miss	Scullery maid	Woldringfold	
Ivalls Alice Mrs (widow)	Cook	Brook Farm	
Jackson Winifred Mrs	Domestic duties	Thornden Lodge	
Jackson Marjorie	At school	Thornden Lodge	
Jakeman Clara Miss	Lady's Companion	Barnfield	

Name	Occupation	Residence	Comment
Jeal Grace Mrs	Housewife	Malvenhurst	
Jeffries Bessie Miss	Children's Nurse	Woldringfold	
Jeffs Emma Miss	Cook	Hill House Farm	
Jester Arthur Mr	Cowman/Bailiff	Old Woldringfold	
Jester Clara Mrs	Domestic duties	Old Woldringfold	
Jester Hazel	At school	Old Woldringfold	
Jester Myrtle	At school	Old Woldringfold	
Jester Mary Mrs (widow)	Domestic duties	6 Huntscroft Gardens	
Jester Charles Mr	Under Gardener	6 Huntscroft Gardens	
Jester Fanny Miss	Domestic duties	6 Huntscroft Gardens	
Jester John Mr	Farm Labourer	6 Huntscroft Gardens	
Johnson Ivy Miss	Domestic Servant (boots)	Eastridge	
Johnson Rose Miss	Housemaid	Eastridge	
Johnston George Mr	Cowman	Oakendene Farm Cottage	
Johnston Joseph Mr	Dairy Farmer	Coopers	
Johnston Hilda Mrs	Domestic duties	Coopers	
Johnston Vernon Mr	Assisting farmer	Coopers	
Jonas George Mr	Odd job man	Ivorys	
Jones David Mr	Butler	Eastridge	
Jones Ernest Mr	Head Gardener	The Gardens, Ivorys	ARP Warden
Jones Lucy Mrs	Domestic duties	The Gardens, Ivorys	
Jones David	Under school age (2 years)	The Gardens, Ivorys	
Jones Thomas Mr	Carter/Cowman	Chatfields Farm Cottages	
Jones Eliza Mrs	Domestic duties	Chatfields Farm Cottages	
Jones David Mr	Under school age (1 year)	Chatfields Farm Cottages	
Jordan Marie Mrs	Housewife	Clock House Farm	Evacuee
Jordan Patrick	At school	Clock House Farm	Evacuee
Kassner Edward Mr	Physician	Gorsedean, Mill Lane	
Kelly Gerald Mr	Stud Groom	1 Smiths Cross Cottage	

Name	Occupation	Residence	Comment
Kelly Prudence Mrs	Domestic duties	1 Smiths Cross Cottage	
Kemp-Welch Sir George	Company Director	Eastridge	
Kemp-Welch Lady D	Domestic duties	Eastridge	
Kemp Margaret	At school	Bulls Bridge Cottage	Evacuee
Kemp William	At school	Coopers Cottage	Evacuee
Kendall Harold Mr	Farm Labourer	South Lodge Stables, Lwr Beeding	
Kennedy Albert Mr	General Works Manager	Potters Green	
Kennedy Helen Mrs	Domestic duties	Potters Green	
Kennedy Helen Miss	Domestic duties	Potters Green	
Kensett Jonathan Mr	Farm Carter (retired)	Violets Cottage, Lwr Beeding	
Kensett Irene Mrs	Domestic duties	Violets Cottage, Lwr Beeding	
Kerr-Jones Theophilus Cpt	Engineer	Wythe	
Kerr-Jones Florence Mrs	Domestic duties	Wythe	
Ketley David	At school	The Wish	Evacuee
Ketley Derek	At school	The Wish	Evacuee
Keyse Albrecht Mr	Butler	Cowfold Lodge Cottage	
Keywood Agnes Mrs (widow)	Domestic duties	2 Elm Grove	
Keywood Joan	At school	2 Elm Grove	
Kidman Monica Mrs	Private means	Longhouse	
King Elizabeth Mrs (widow)	Incapacitated	West Lodge, Woldringfold	
King Lily Mrs (widow)	Domestic duties	5 New Cottages, Mill Lane	
King Kenneth Mr	Gardener	5 New Cottages, Mill Lane	
King Nelson Mr	Farm Labourer	Little Burnt House	
King Elsie Miss	Domestic duties	Little Burnt House	
King Nelson Mr	Carrier	8 Council Cottages	Special constable
King Ethel Mrs	Domestic duties	8 Council Cottages	
King Margaret Miss	Nursery Probationer	Woldringfold	
King Wendy Miss	Nursery Probationer	Woldringfold	
Kingsland Richard Mr	Retired	Bunton	

Name	Occupation	Residence	Comment
Kingsland Amelia Mrs	Domestic duties	Bunton	
Kingsland Leonard Mr	Gardener	Bunton	
Knight Alban Mr	Gardener	North Stone Cottages	
Knight Florence Mrs	Domestic duties	North Stone Cottages	
Knight James Mr	Head Cowman	Chatfields Farm	
Knight Beatrice Mrs	Domestic duties	Chatfields Farm	
Women's Land Army			
Knight William Mr	Cowman	North Stone	
Knight Alice Mrs	Domestic duties	North Stone	
Laker Ernest Mr	Baker's Roundsman	Gratwick Cottages	
Laker Nellie Mrs	Domestic duties	Gratwick Cottages	
Laker Bertha Mrs	Domestic duties	Gratwick Cottages	
Laker Gordon	At school	Gratwick Cottages	
Laker Michael	At school	Gratwick Cottages	
Laker Raymond Mr	Labourer/Gardener	Gratwick Cottages	
Laker William Mr	Engine Driver	5 Woodville Terrace	
Laker Clara Mrs	Domestic duties	5 Woodville Terrace	
Laker Arthur	At school	5 Woodville Terrace	
Langridge Albert Mr	Council Roadman	Singers Cottage	
Langridge Mary Mrs	Domestic duties	Singers Cottage	
Langridge Albert Mr	Wood Working Machinist	Willingdale	
Langridge Alice Mrs	Domestic duties	Willingdale	
Langridge Annie Miss	Laundress	Banfield Cottages	
Langridge Robert Mr	Builder's Foreman	1 Tollgate Cottages	
Langridge Ellen Mrs	Domestic duties	1 Tollgate Cottages	
Langridge Jesse Mr	Gardener	1 Tollgate Cottages	
Langridge Reginald	At school	1 Tollgate Cottages	
Larby Frederick Mr	GPO Overseer	Mill Lane	
Larby Maude Mrs	Domestic duties	Mill Lane	
Larkin Margaret	At school	Oakendene	Evacuee
Laury Frank Mr	Kitchen Gardener	1 Drewitts Cottages	
Laury Mabel Mrs	Domestic duties	1 Drewitts Cottages	

Name	Occupation	Residence	Comment
Lawrence Edith Miss	Paid Domestic	Sadlers	
Lewis Barbara Miss	Domestic duties	New Steyne House	
Lewis Edith Miss	Children's Nurse	Oakendene	
Lidbetter Arthur Mr	Gardener	Hill Farm Cottages	
Lidbetter Aida Mrs	Domestic duties	Hill Farm Cottages	
Lieber Annie Mrs	Domestic duties	Rosslyn	
Lindfield George Mr	Gardener	23 Mill Lane, Lwr Beeding	
Lindfield Rosa Mrs	Domestic duties	23 Mill Lane, Lwr Beeding	
Lindfield Basil Mr	Bricklayer	23 Mill Lane, Lwr Beeding	
Lindfield Elsie Miss	Domestic duties	23 Mill Lane, Lwr Beeding	
Lithgow Samuel Mr	Land Agent	Peppersgate	
Lithgow Rachel Mrs	Domestic duties	Peppersgate	
Lithgow Esther	At school	Peppersgate	
Loader Violet	At school	2 Elm Grove	Evacuee
Longhurst Albert Mr	Farm Labourer	Pound House	
Longhurst Alice Mrs	Domestic duties	Pound House	
Longhurst Frederick Mr	Builder's Labourer	Pound House	
Loten Henry Mr (widower)	Gardener	North Lodge	
Loten Frances Miss	Domestic duties	North Lodge	
Lovegrove Winifred Mrs	Farmer	Gratwick Farm	
Lovett-Cameron Capt.	Private means	Brookhill House	
Lovett-Cameron Mrs	Domestic duties	Brookhill House	
Luff Raymond Mr	Builder's Labourer	The Bungalow, Henfield Road	
Luxford Bessie Mrs (widow)	Domestic duties	Tremosa	
Macdonald Isabella Miss	State Registered Nurse	Lydford	
Maidlow Beatrice Mrs	Domestic duties	Chatfields Farm	Evacuee
Maidlow Valerie	Under school age (4 years)	Chatfields Farm	Evacuee
Malboy James Mr	Waiter	Banfield Cottages	

Name	Occupation	Residence	Comment
Malyon William Mr	Gardener (retired)	Potters House	
Malyon Emily Mrs	Domestic duties	Potters House	
Malyon George Mr	Motor Mechanic	Potters House	
Mansbridge Harriet Mrs (wid)	Domestic duties	1 Margaret Cottages	
Marchant Martha Miss	Incapacitated	2 Huntscroft Gardens	
Marsden Patricia	At school	Bunton	Evacuee
Marshall William Mr	Bank Messenger	Wood Grange	
Marshall Dorothy Mrs	Domestic duties	Wood Grange	
Martin Frederick Mr	Cowman	Potters Cottages	
Martin Dorothy Mrs	Domestic duties	Potters Cottages	
Matlock Sheila	At school	2 Elm Grove	Evacuee
Matthews Annie Miss	Maid	Cowfold Lodge	
Matthews Mark Mr	Dairy Farmer	Wilcox Farm	
Matthews Alice Mrs	Domestic duties	Wilcox Farm	
Matthews Mary	At school	Wilcox Farm	
Matthews Thomas Dr	Doctor	The Red House	
Matthews Doris Mrs	Domestic duties	The Red House	
May Charles Mr	Cowman	Little Brook	
May Emily Mrs	Domestic duties	Little Brook	
Maynard Percy Mr	Grocer's Assistant	Wood Grange	
Maynard Lucy Mrs	Domestic duties	Wood Grange	
McCormack Florence Miss	Paid Domestic	Clock House	
McHara Isabel Miss	Parlourmaid	Woldringfold	
McIntyre Harold Mr	Dairy Farmer	Brownings	
McIntyre Mabel Mrs	Farm work	Brownings	
McPherson Isabella Miss	Domestic duties	The Cottage, Clock House	
Medhurst Percy Mr	Builder's Labourer	Woodville	
Medhurst Frances Mrs	Domestic duties	Woodville	

Name	Occupation	Residence	Comment
Millham Maurice Mr	Contractor's Labourer	Stonefield Cottages	
Millham Bessie Mrs	Domestic duties	Stonefield Cottages	
Millichamp Albert Mr	Nurse	Potters Green	
Mills Thomas Mr	Painter	1 Oakfield Cottages	ARP Warden
Mills Mary Mrs	Domestic duties	1 Oakfield Cottages	
Mills William Mr	Labourer	Archers	
Minihane Albert Mr	Blacksmith	5 Oakfield Cottages	
Minihane Nellie Mrs	Domestic duties	5 Oakfield Cottages	
Minihane James Mr	Gardener	5 Oakfield Cottages	
Minihane Elizabeth	At school	5 Oakfield Cottages	
Mist James Mr	Agricultural Carpenter	5 Mill Lane, Lwr Beeding	
Mist Violet Mrs	Domestic duties	5 Mill Lane, Lwr Beeding	
Mist Tony Mr	Domestic duties	5 Mill Lane, Lwr Beeding	
Mitchell Caroline Miss	Dressmaker	4 Elm Grove	
Mitchell Horace Mr	Gardener	Church Gate	Special Constable
Mitchell Elizabeth Mrs (widow)	Domestic duties	Church Gate	
Mitchell John Mr	Road Labourer	Church Terrace	
Mitchell Evelyn Mrs	Domestic duties	Church Terrace	
Mitchell Kenneth	At school	Church Terrace	
Mitchell Mary Mrs (widow)	Cook	Wood Grange	
Mitchell Mary Mrs (widow)	Domestic duties	4 Elm Grove	
Mitchell William Mr	Groom	6 Elm Grove	
Mobsby Victoria Mrs (widow)	Domestic duties	6 Council Cottages	
Moody James Mr	Scullery Boy	Ivorys	
Moore Frank Mr	Estate Labourer	Parkminster Lodge	
Moore Annie Mrs	Domestic duties	Parkminster Lodge	

Name	Occupation	Residence	Comment
Moore Reginald Mr	Gardener	Brookhill Lodge	
Moore Grace Mrs	Domestic duties	Brookhill Lodge	
Moore Bernard	At school	Brookhill Lodge	
Moore Rosemary	At school	Brookhill Lodge	
Moore Wesley Mr	Builder's Bricklayer	12 Hillside, Lwr Beeding	
Moore Mary Mrs	Domestic duties	12 Hillside, Lwr Beeding	
Morris Nellie Mrs	Domestic duties	13 Homeleigh, Lwr Beeding	
Morrissey Joan Miss	Nurse	Woldringfold	
Moulton Arthur Mr	House Painter	10 Mill Lane, Lwr Beeding	
Moulton Florence Mrs	Domestic duties	10 Mill Lane, Lwr Beeding	
Muggeridge Henry Mr	Tractor Driver	14 Mount Pleasant	
Muggeridge Lottie Mrs	Domestic duties	14 Mount Pleasant	
Muggeridge Mary Mrs	Domestic duties	14 Mount Pleasant	
Muir James Mr	Herdsman/ Farm Hand	Ivorys Farm	
Muir Rose Mrs	Dairy and Poultry Hand	Ivorys Far	
Mullett William Mr	Farmer	Dragon's Farm	
Mullett Henrietta Mrs	Domestic duties	Dragon's Farm	
Mullett John Mr	Farm Carter	Dragon's Farm	
Mullett Victor Mr	Cowman	Dragon's Farm	Special Constable
Mullett Violet Miss	Domestic duties	Dragon's Farm	
Muncey Frank Mr	Caretaker	The Village Hall	Police Reserve
Muncey Ethel Mrs	Domestic duties	The Village Hall	
Munro Richard Mr	Merchant Banker	Oakendene	
Munro Lilian Mrs	Domestic duties	Oakendene	Women's Land Army
Murphy Ellen Mrs	Domestic duties	Frithlands	Evacuee
Murphy Margaret	At school	Frithlands	Evacuee
Murphy Ann	Under school age (8 months)	Frithlands	Evacuee
Musso Heather Miss	Domestic duties	Lydford	
Muzzell George Mr	Farm Labourer	Bulls Bridge	
Muzzell Kate Mrs	Domestic duties	Bulls Bridge	

Name	Occupation	Residence	Comment
Neilson George Mr	British Army retired	Eastridge	
Neilson Agnes Mrs	Domestic duties	Eastridge	
Newman Raymond Mr	Farm Carter	2 White Houses	
Newman Sarah Mrs	Domestic duties	2 White Houses	
Newman Moses Mr	Retired	2 White Houses	
Newman Edith Miss	Jobbing Domestic	2 White Houses	
Nicklin Jessie Mrs	Domestic duties	Longhouse Lodge	
Noakes Herbert Mr	Farm Hand	2 Oakendene New Cottages	
Noakes Gertrude Mrs	Domestic duties	2 Oakendene New Cottages	
Norris Robert Mr	Chef's Assistant	Ivorys	
O'Connor Patrick	At school	Hill Farm Cottages	Evacuee
Oliver George Mr	Baker	Bolney Mead	
Oliver Sarah Mrs (widow)	Domestic duties	Bolney Mead	
O'Reilly Dorothy Mrs	Domestic duties	Hare and Hounds	
Overbury Gladys Mrs	Domestic duties	South Lodge Cottage, Lwr Beeding	
Packham Arthur Mr	Bricklayer	Hazlebank	
Packham Margaret Mrs	Domestic duties	Hazlebank	
Packham Eric Mr	Gardener	Hazlebank	
Packham Ernest Mr	Builder's Labourer	2 Oakfield Cottages	
Packham Agnes Mrs	Domestic duties	2 Oakfield Cottages	
Packham James Mr	Council Labourer	Parkminster	
Packham Louisa Miss	Home domestic	Parkminster	
Page Eric Mr	Dairy Farmer	Homelands Farm	
Page Hilda Mrs	Domestic duties	Homelands Farm	
Page Derek	At school	Homelands Farm	
Papa Luigi Mr	Hairdresser	Mockford	ARP warden
Papa Kathleen Mrs	Domestic duties	Mockford	
Papa Gloria Mrs	Hairdresser (retired)	Mockford	
Papa Josephine Mrs	Domestic duties	Mockford	
Papa Monica	At school	Mockford	

Name	Occupation	Residence	Comment
Parsons Arthur Mr	Market Garden Foreman	20 Mill Lane, Lwr Beeding	
Parsons Phyllis Mrs	Domestic duties	20 Mill Lane, Lwr Beeding	
Parsons Charles Mr	Bricklayer	Baldwins Cottage	
Parsons Winifred Mrs	Domestic duties	Baldwins Cottage	
Parsons Elizabeth Miss	Domestic duties	3 Margaret Cottages	
Parsons Frederick Mr	Chimney Sweep	Homefields	
Parsons Ethel Mrs	Domestic duties	Homefileds	
Parsons Harry Mr	Farm Hand	South Lodge Stables	ARP Warden
Parsons Cecilia Mrs	Domestic duties	South Lodge Stables	
Parsons Horace Mr	Gardener	Aglands	
Parsons Ethel Mrs	Domestic duties	Aglands	
Parsons Jesse Mr	Farm Labourer	1 White Houses	
Parsons Ellen Mrs	Domestic duties	1 White Houses	
Parsons Jesse Mr (widower)	Retired	4 Margaret Cottages	
Parsons Joan Miss	Kitchen Maid	Brookhill House	
Parsons John Mr	Farm Carter (retired)	Aglands	
Parsons Charlotte Mrs	Domestic duties	Aglands	
Parsons Robert Mr	Head Gardener	St Michaels	
Parsons Gwendoline Mrs	Domestic duties	St Michaels	
Parsons Walter Mr	Council Roadman	Church Terrace	
Parsons Esther Mrs	Domestic duties	Church Terrace	
Parsons Jean	At school	Church Terrace	
Parsons William Mr	Farm Carter	4 New Cottages, Mill Lane	
Parsons Emily Mrs	Domestic duties	4 New Cottages, Mill Lane	
Parsons Walter Mr	Gardener	6 Elm Grove	
Parsons Alice Mrs	Domestic duties	6 Elm Grove	
Patching Eliza Mrs (widow)	Domestic duties	Picts Cottages	

Name	Occupation	Residence	Comment
Paull Harold Mr	Farm Carter	8 Mill Lane	
Paull Evelyn Mrs	Domestic duties	8 Mill Lane	
Paull Terrence Mr	House Painter	8 Mill Lane	
Paulton Florence Mrs	Domestic duties	8 Council Cottages	Evacuee
Pavey Dorothy Miss	Cook/Housekeeper	Brookhill House	
Peacock Sarah Miss	Kitchenmaid	South Lodge, Lwr Beeding	
Peacock Walter Mr	Grocer	Jersey House	Special Constable
Peacock Louise Mrs	Domestic duties	Jersey House	
Peacock Louisa	Domestic duties	Jersey House	
Pearson Alice Mrs	Domestic servant	Wallhurst Manor	
Pengelly Eric Mr	Butler	Clock House	
Perdigao Alice Miss	Domestic Maid	Ivorys	
Peters Annie Miss	Laundress	Banfield Cottages	
Petley Harry Mr	Butler	The Bothy, South Lodge, Lwr Beeding	
Pinnock Sylvia Mrs	Housewife	Malvenhurst	
Plumbley James Mr	Salesman (tobacco)	Averies House	
Plumbley Violette Mrs	Domestic duties	Averies House	
Pointing Sydney Mr	Bus Conductor	Wallhurst Lodge	
Pointing Alice Mrs	Domestic duties	Wallhurst Lodge	
Pollard Frederick Mr	Head Cowman	Gratwick Cottages	
Pollard Alice Mrs	Domestic duties	Gratwick Cottages	
Pollard Winifred Miss	Domestic duties	Gratwick Cottages	
Pollard Joy Miss	Domestic duties	Gratwick Farm	
Porter Sidney Mr	Lodge Keeper	Parkminster Lodge	
Porter Beatrice Mrs	Domestic duties	Parkminster Lodge	
Potter Gertrude Mrs	Domestic duties	Ingleside	
Poulton Kenneth	At school	North Stone	Evacuee
Powell Eleanor Miss	Nurse	Ivorys	

Name	Occupation	Residence	Comment
Powell Frederick Mr	Pigman	15 Mount Pleasant	
Powell Evelyn Mrs	Domestic duties	15 Mount Pleasant	
Powell Geoffrey	At school	15 Mount Pleasant	
Powell Percy Mr	Milkman/Farm Labourer	15 Mount Pleasant	
Pratt Charles Mr	Shepherd	Pound House	
Pratt Daisy Mrs	Domestic duties	Pound House	
Prett Sarah Miss	Paid Domestic	Clock House	
Prestridge Albert Mr	Farm Labourer	Oakendene Cottage	
Pritchard Dorette	At school	4 Woodville Terrace	Evacuee
Pritchard Ernest	At school	Jersey House	Evacuee
Pummell Walter Mr	Motor Mechanic	7 Council Cottages	
Pummell Grace Mrs	Domestic duties	7 Council Cottages	
Quick Reginald Mr	Headmaster	St Peter's School	Deputy Controller ARP
Quick Rosalind Mrs	Domestic duties	St Peter's School	
Radford Frederick Mr	Kitchen Gardener	Gratfields	
Radford Annie Mrs	Domestic duties	Gratfields	
Radford Patience	At school	Gratfields	
Radford Victor	At school	Gratfields	
Ralls Reginald Mr	Dairy Farmer	Maryland Farm	
Ralls Emily Mrs	Domestic duties	Maryland Farm	
Ralls Peter	At school	Maryland Farm	
Ralls Pamela Miss	Domestic duties	Maryland Farm	
Ralph Mary Mrs	Domestic duties	The Cottage, Eastlands Lane	
Ralph Elizabeth	Under school age (3 years)	The Cottage, Eastlands Lane	
Ralph Minnie Mrs	Domestic duties	6 Church Path	
Ralph Fanny Miss	Domestic servant	6 Church Path	
Rampton Olive Mrs	Domestic duties	12 Hillside, Lwr Beeding	
Randall Henry Mr	Stud Groom	Thornden (Stables)	
Rayner Bertie Mr	Butler	Ivorys	

Name	Occupation	Residence	Comment
Reed Ernest Mr	Stud Groom	Brook Farm Cottages	
Reed Margaret Mrs	Domestic duties	Brook Farm Cottages	
Rew Edward Mr	Chauffeur	3 South Lodge Cottage, Lwr Beeding	
Rew Molly Mrs	Domestic duties	3 South Lodge Cottage, Lwr Beeding	
Rew Phyllis Miss	Teacher	3 South Lodge Cottage, Lwr Beeding	
Rice Margaret Mrs (widow)	Retired	2 Margaret Cottages	
Richardson Edward Mr	Blacksmith and Farrier	16 Ivy Cottages, Crabtree	
Richardson Elsie Mrs	Domestic duties	16 Ivy Cottages, Crabtree	
Riley Sarah Miss	Cook	6 New Cottages, Mill Lane	
Roberts Frederick Mr	Managing Director	Cowfold Lodge	
Roberts Adelaide Mrs	Domestic duties	Cowfold Lodge	
Roberts James Mr	Lorry Driver	1 Elm Grove	
Roberts Katherine Mrs	Domestic duties	1 Elm Grove	
Roberts Frederick Mr	Lorry Driver	1 Elm Grove	
Roberts John Mr	Builder (retired)	Ellerslie	
Robertson Frank Mr	Pensioner	6 Elm Grove	
Roe Alfred Mr	Chauffeur (retired)	Coopers Cottage	
Roe Beatrice Mrs	Domestic duties	Coopers Cottage	
Roe Cyril	At school	Coopers Cottage	
Roe Sarah	At school	Coopers Cottage	
Roe Frederick Mr	Tobacco Sales Manager	Wood Grange	
Roe Winifred Mrs	Domestic duties	Wood Grange	
Romanin Rosa Miss	Domestic Maid	Cowfold Lodge	
Rooney Dennis Mr	Horse Breaker	Rosslyn	
Rooney Katherine Mrs	Domestic duties	Rosslyn	
Rooney Michael	Under school age (4 years)	Rosslyn	
Ross Mary Mrs	Domestic duties	Longhouse (Garage)	
Ross Jean	At school	Longhouse (Garage)	
Ross Barbara	At school	Longhouse (Garage)	

Name	Occupation	Residence	Comment
Rouch Kate	Private Means	The Vicarage	
Rowe Helen Miss	Trained Nurse	Allfreys	
Rowell Elsie Miss	Children's Nurse	The Red House	
Runnalls Oliver Mr	Dairy Farmer	Southlands Farm	
Runnalls Queenie Mrs	Domestic duties	Southlands Farm	
Runnalls Ada Mrs	Domestic duties	Southlands Farm	
Runnalls Gloria	At school	Southlands Farm	
Runnalls Sheila	At school	Southlands Farm	
Russell Benjamin Mr	Garden Labourer	Lydford Cottage	
Russell Ethel Mrs	Domestic duties	Lydford Cottage	
Russell Elsie Miss	Domestic duties	Lydford Cottage	
Rutledge John Mr	Agricultural Worker	22 Mill Lane, Lwr Beeding	
Rutledge Elizabeth Mrs	Domestic duties	22 Mill Lane, Lwr Beeding	
Rutledge Michael	Under school age (3 years)	22 Mill lane, Lwr Beeding	
Rutledge Mary Mrs (widow)	Domestic duties	Kings Barn	
Rymell William Mr	Retired	6 Margaret Cottages	
Rymell Charlotte Mrs	Domestic duties	6 Margaret Cottages	
Salter Harry Mr	Farm Foreman	Mockford	
Salter Marjorie Mrs	Domestic duties	Mockford	
Salter Richard	Under school age (3 months)	Mockford	
Sandberg Rev William	Vicar	The Vicarage	
Sandberg Ethel Mrs	Domestic Duties	The Vicarage	
Sanders Ernest Mr	Carpenter	Old Steyne House	
Sanders Vida Mrs	Domestic duties	Old Steyne House	
Sanderson Florence Mrs	Domestic duties	North Lodge	
Sanderson Mary Mrs (widow)	Domestic duties	Karemore, Parkminster	
Sanderson William Mr	Chauffeur	Parkminster	
Sanderson Edith Mrs	Domestic duties	Parkminster	
Sanderson John	At school	Parkminster	
Sanderson Peter	At school	Parkminster	

Name	Occupation	Residence	Comment
Saunders Rose Mrs	Domestic duties	Bulls Bridge Cottage	
Savegar Charles Mr (widower)	Head Gardener	The Lodge, South Lodge, Lwr Beeding	
Savegar Evelyn Miss	Domestic duties	The Lodge, South Lodge, Lwr Beeding	
Sawyer Constance Miss	Housemaid	Brownings	
Sayers Charlie Mr	Bricklayer	Picts Cottages	
Sayers Sarah Mrs	Domestic duties	Picts Cottages	
Sayers Gordon	At school	Picts Cottages	
Sayers Christopher Mr	Dairy Farmer	Northfields	
Sayers Sylvia Mrs	Domestic duties	Northfields	
Sayers Christopher Mr	Farm Labourer (retired)	High Hurst Cottages	
Sayers Alice Mrs	Domestic duties	High Hurst Cottages	
Sayers May Miss	Domestic duties	High Hurst Cottages	
Sayers Ellen Miss	Housemaid	Hill House Farm	
Sayers Olive Miss	Parlour Maid	Allfreys	
Sayers William Mr	Postman	4 Council Cottages	
Sayers Alice Mrs	Domestic duties	4 Council Cottages	
Sayers William Mr	Chauffeur	Oakendene Cottage	
Sayers Florence Mrs	Domestic duties	Oakendene Cottage	
Scutt Kate Miss	Domestic duties	11 Hillside, Lwr Beeding	
Seal Lillian Mrs (widow)	Domestic duties	North Stone	
Searle William Mr	Farm Carter	11 Hillside, Lwr Beeding	
Sedlery Dorothy Mrs	Domestic duties	Barnfield Lodge	Evacuee
Sendall Frank Mr	Café Caterer/ Poultry Farmer	Singers	
Shannon John Mr	Police Constable (retired)	Allfreys Cottages	
Shannon Evelyn Mrs	Domestic duties	Allfreys Cottages	
Shannon John Mr	Motor Mechanic	Allfreys Cottages	
Shannon Wilfred	At school	Allfreys Cottages	

Name	Occupation	Residence	Comment
Sherlock William Mr	Builder's Labourer	7 Mill Lane, Lwr Beeding	
Sherlock Dorothy Mrs	Domestic duties	7 Mill Lane, Lwr Beeding	
Sherlock George	At school	7 Mill lane, Lwr Beeding	
Sherlock Winifred Miss	Paid Domestic	The Stores	
Shier Archibald Mr	Dairy Farmer	Capons Hill Farm	
Shier Florence Mrs	Domestic duties	Capons Hill Farm	
Short Florence Miss	Housemaid	Woldringfold	
Shrubb William Mr	Postman	1 Glenthorne	
Shrubb Margaret Mrs	Domestic duties	1 Glenthorne	
Sillence Florence Miss	Matron (Resident Home)	South Lodge, Lwr Beeding	
Silver Leslie	At school	Malvenhurst	Evacuee
Simcock Angela Miss	Private means	Barrington Cottage	Probationer Red Cross
Simmonds Robert Mr	Licensee	Hare and Hounds	
Simmonds Ann Mrs	Domestic duties	Hare and Hounds	
Slocombe Frederick Mr	Assistant Schoolmaster	West View	
Slocombe Margaret Mrs	Domestic duties	West View	
Slocombe Brian	Under school age (1 year)	West View	
Smith Constance Mrs	Domestic duties	Ivorys Lodge	
Smith Edwin Mr	Retired	1 Council Cottages	
Smith Frederick Mr	Carpenter/Joiner	3 Council Cottages	
Smith Elsie Mrs	Domestic duties	3 Council Cottages	
Smith George Mr	Gardener	33 New Cottages, Lwr Beeding	Special Constable
Smith Rose Mrs	Domestic duties	33 New Cottages, Lwr Beeding	
Smith Derek	At school	33 New Cottages, Lwr Beeding	
Smith Irene	At school	Hill Farm Cottages	Evacuee
Smith Jessie Mrs	Domestic duties	North Lodge	

Name	Occupation	Residence	Comment
Smith Maureen	At school	Potters Green	Evacuee
Smyth Dolly Miss	Bakery Shop Help	The Bakery	
Southon Frank Mr	Herdsman	Godshill Farm	
Southon Edith Mrs	Domestic duties	Godshill Farm	
Southon Ronald	At school	Godshill Farm	
Sparks Young Mr	Woodman/Sawyer	Taintfield Cottages	
Sparks Tryphena Miss	Domestic duties	Taintfield Cottages	
Sparks Alexander	Under school age (8 months)	Taintfield Cottages	
Spencer Eugenie Mrs	Domestic duties	Stable Cottage, Clock House	
Spinks Robert Mr	Hotel Proprietor	The Red Lion	
Spinks Alice Mrs	Domestic duties	The Red Lion	
Spinks Mary Miss	Domestic duties	The Red Lion	
Sprinks Oliver Mr	Electrical Storekeeper (ret'd)	The Red Lion	
Sprinks Ellen Mrs	Domestic duties	The Red Lion	
Sprinks William Mr	Grocer	The Stores	
Sprinks Elenor Miss	Domestic duties	The Stores	
Standen Henry Mr	Farm Labourer	Oakendene Farm	
Stanford William Mr	Cowman	21 Mill lane, Lwr Beeding	
Stanford Kate Mrs	Domestic duties	21 Mill Lane, Lwr Beeding	
Stening Elizabeth Miss	Private means	Burnt House	
Stevens Sheila Mrs	Domestic duties	Wallhurst Lodge	
Steward Sidney Mr	Gardener	4 Drewitts Cottages	
Steward Beatrice Mrs	Domestic duties	4 Drewitts Cottages	
Stocks Gladys Mrs	Domestic duties	Allfreys (Garage)	
Stoner Edmund Mr	Gardener	2 Tollgate Cottages	
Stoner Lucy Mrs	Domestic duties	2 Tollgate Cottages	
Stoner Edward Mr	Coal Carman	Old Shop Cottage	
Stoner Frederick Mr	Estate Hand	Old Woldringfold	
Stoner Ethel Mrs	Domestic duties	Old Woldringfold	

Name	Occupation	Residence	Comment
Stoner George Mr	Woodman	The Ferns, Mill Lane, Lwr Beeding	
Stoner Matilda Mrs	Domestic duties	The Ferns, Mill Lane, Lwr Beeding	
Stoner George Mr	Agricultural Labourer	The Ferns, Mill Lane, Lwr Beeding	
Stoner George Mr	Labourer (retired)	1 Mill Lane, Lwr Beeding	
Stoner Mary Mrs	Domestic duties	1 Mill Lane, Lwr Beeding	
Stoner Alice Miss	Domestic duties	1 Mill Lane, Lwr Beeding	
Sturgell Herbert Mr	Cowman	Parkminster Farm	
Sturgell Ada Mrs	Housekeeper	Parkminster Farm	
Sykes Rose Mrs	Domestic duties	Bulls Bridge Cottage	
Sykes Jeanette Miss	Domestic duties	Bulls Bridge Cottage	
Symmonds Henry Mr	Carpenter	2 Woodville Terrace	ARP Warden
Symmonds Dorothy Mrs	Domestic duties	2 Woodville Terrace	
Tabutt Nathan Mr	Groom	Thornden (Stables)	
Tagliavin Hilda Mrs	Domestic duties	Brook Farm Cottages	
Tarrant Derrick	At school	Little Burnt House	Evacuee
Taylor John	At school	Holmstead	Evacuee
Telford Walter Mr	Dog Trainer	Wallhurst Manor	
Telford Sarah Mrs	Domestic duties	Wallhurst Manor	
Telling Elsie Miss	Cook	Woldringfold	
Thomas Annie Miss	Housemaid	Longhouse	
Thomas George Mr	Baker's Assistant	The Bakery	
Thomas Reginald Mr	Farmer	Crateman's Farm	
Thomas Hilda Mrs	Domestic duties	Crateman's Farm	
Thomas Ivan	At school	Crateman's Farm	
Thompson Dorothy Mrs	Domestic duties	Eastridge Lodge	
Thompson Joy Miss	Clerk	2 South Lodge Cottage, Lwr Beeding	
Thorns Harriet Mrs (widow)	Invalid	1 Margaret Cottages	

Name	Occupation	Residence	Comment
Thorns Henry Mr	General Labourer	Mockford	
Thorns Ada Mrs	Domestic duties	Mockford	
Thorns Albert Mr	Builder's Labourer	Mockford	
Thrussell Sidney Mr	Estate Laundry work	Laundry House, Mill Lane	
Thrussell Annie Mrs	Estate Laundry work	Laundry House, Mill Lane	
Thrussell George	At school	Laundry House, Mill Lane	
Thurston Flora Mrs	Domestic duties	2 Mill Lane, Lwr Beeding	
Tibbles Beatrice Mrs	Domestic duties	3 Drewitts Cottages	Evacuee
Tibbles Peter	Under school age (4 years)	3 Drewitts Cottages	Evacuee
Tidey Frederick Mr	Garage Proprietor	Bridgwater	Special Constable
Tidey Henrietta Mrs	Domestic duties	Bridgwater	
Tidey Elizabeth Mrs (widow)	Incapacitated	5 New Cottages, Mill Lane	
Tindall Louis Mr	Commercial Clerk	Wyndham	
Tindall Kate Mrs	Domestic duties	Wyndham	
Tindall Phyllis Mrs	Teacher	Wyndham	
Townsend Renee Miss	Housemaid	Drewitts	
Townsend Stephen Mr	Poultry Farmer	Banfield Cottages	
Townsend Beatrice Mrs	Domestic duties	Banfield Cottages	
Townsend Norman Mr	Gardener Handyman	Banfield Cottages	
Townsend Kenneth	At school	Banfield Cottages	
Trenaman Sidney Mr	Police Officer (retired)	Cottlands	ARP Warden
Trenaman Ethel Mrs	Domestic duties	Cottlands	
Trigg Roy Mr	Farmer	Parkminster Farm	
Trimby Leslie Mr	Gardener	The Bothy, South Lodge, Lwr Beeding	
Trimby Florence Mrs	Domestic duties	The Bothy, South Lodge, Lwr Beeding	
Trott May Mrs (widow)	Domestic duties	Bunton	WVS
Trotter Elizabeth Mrs (widow)	Private means	Peppersgate	
Trusty Kate Miss	Domestic servant	The Vicarage	

Name	Occupation	Residence	Comment
Tuck Alfred Mr	Carpenter	Willcox Cottage	
Tuck Kate Mrs	Domestic duties	Willcox Cottage	
Tuck Frederick Mr	Cowman	Ridgelands Bungalow	
Tuck Rebecca Mrs	Domestic duties	Ridgelands Bungalow	
Tullett Elizabeth Mrs (widow)	Incapacitated	Gratfields	
Tullett Mary Mrs (widow)	Domestic duties	Cottlands Platts	
Tullett Roland Mr	Managing farm	Cottlands Platts	
Tullett William Mr	Farm Foreman	Ivorys Lodge	
Tullett Elizabeth Mrs	Domestic duties	Ivorys Lodge	
Underhill Hilda Miss	Governess	Capons Farm	WVS
Upham Emily Miss	Dressmaker	South Lodge, Lwr Beeding	
Vinall William Mr	Bricklayer (retired)	South View, Mill Lane, Lwr Beeding	
Vinall Mary Mrs	Domestic duties	South View, Mill Lane, Lwr Beeding	
Wackman Anna Mrs	Incapacitated	Glen Lyn	
Wadey Alice Mrs	Music Teacher	North Stone Cottages	
Wadey James Mr	Builder Joiner	4 Huntscroft Gardens	
Wadey Elizabeth Mrs	Domestic duties	4 Huntscroft Gardens	
Wakeford Philip Mr	Head Cowman	Trenchmore Cottage	
Wakeford Rose Mrs	Cook	Trenchmore Cottage	
Walder Frank Mr	Cowman	Drewitts Lodge	
Walder Grace Mrs	Domestic duties	Drewitts Lodge	
Walder Eliza Mrs (widow)	Domestic duties	Drewitts Lodge	
Walder William Mr	Builder/Decorator	Church Farm House	
Walder Alice Mrs	Domestic duties	Church Farm House	
Walder William Mr	Painter	Oakleigh	
Walder Irene Mrs	Domestic duties	Oakleigh	
Walker Bridget Mrs	Domestic duties	Ivorys	Evacuee
Walls Henry Mr	Farm Carter	High Hurst Cottages	
Walls Margaret Mrs	Domestic duties	High Hurst Cottages	

Name	Occupation	Residence	Comment
Walters Arthur Mr	Gardener	Bulls Bridge Cottage	
Walters Annie Mrs	Domestic duties	Bulls Bridge Cottage	
Walters Vera Miss	Domestic duties	Bulls Bridge Cottage	
Ward Elizabeth Miss	Domestic duties	7 Elm Grove	
Ward Catherine Miss	Domestic duties	7 Elm Grove	
Warren Leonard Mr	Butler	Drewitts	
Watling Beatrice Miss	Cook/Housekeeper	South Lodge, Lwr Beeding	
Watson Agnes Mrs (widow)	Domestic duties	Clovelly	
Watson Marjorie Miss	Domestic duties	Clovelly	
Watson Mary Mrs (widow)	Domestic duties	Brook Farm Cottages	
Watson Philip Mr	Cowman and Carter	Bulls Cottage	
Watson Daisy Mrs	Domestic duties	Bulls Cottage	
Watson Philip	Under school age (2 years)	Bulls Cottage	
Watts Hilda Mrs	Domestic duties	Drewitts	
Watts Joy Miss	Housekeeper	Drewitts	
Webster John Mr	General Labourer	6 Mill Lane, Lwr Beeding	
Weiss Ernest Mr	Gardener	Furzefield House	
Weiss Elfrida Mrs	Cook	Furzefield House	
Welch Kathleen Mrs (widow)	Shop Keeper	The Old Shop	
Weller Stanley Mr	Groom	Longhouse	
Weller Eliza Mrs	Housekeeper	Longhouse	
West Alfred Mr	Baker	The Bakery	Special Constable
West Edith Mrs	Domestic duties	The Bakery	
West Michael	At school	The Bakery	
Wheeler Brenda	At school	"Fretridge", Brook Hill	Evacuee
Whelpton Jennifer	Under school age (3 years)	North Lodge	Evacuee
Whitelaw Beatrice Mrs	Domestic duties	Oakcroft	
Whitelaw Doreen Miss	Domestic duties	Oakcroft	

Name	Occupation	Residence	Comment
Wiertz Annie Miss	Shorthand Typist	Ivorys	
Wiggins Martha Mrs (widow)	Householder	Aughamore	
Wiggins Evelyn Miss	Domestic duties	Aughamore	
Wiggins Olive Miss	Private Secretary	Aughamore	
Wilkins Hedley Mr	Managing Director	Barrington Cottage	
Wilkins Lilian Mrs	Domestic duties	Barrington Cottage	
Wilkinson Ada Miss	Domestic service	Oakendene	
Wilkinson Beatrice Miss	Domestic service	Oakendene	
Wilkinson Norah Miss	Domestic service	Oakendene	
Wing Frederick Mr	Grocer's Assistant	Fair View	
Wing Lilian Mrs	Domestic duties	Fair View	
Will Elizabeth Miss	Cook	South Lodge, Lwr Beeding	
Winstanley John Mr	Private, Royal Sussex Regt	2 Rock Cottage	
Winstanley Catherine Mrs	Domestic duties	2 Rock Cottage	
Woyka Maud Mrs	Domestic duties	Furzefield House	Evacuee
Woyka Robert	Under school age (3 years)	Furzefield House	Evacuee
Woodridge Thomas Mr	Gardener	Stable Cottage, Clock House	
Woolven Agnes Miss	Retired (invalid)	Massetts	
Woolven Alfred Mr	Grocer's Carman	3 Elm Grove	
Woolven Gladys Mrs	Domestic duties	3 Elm Grove	
Woolven Arthur Mr	Gardener	The Reading Rooms	
Woolven Maria Mrs	Domestic duties	The Reading Rooms	
Woolven Edward Mr	Grocer's Assistant	1 Huntscroft Gardens	
Woolven Nellie Mrs	Domestic duties	1 Huntscroft Gardens	
Woolven Mary Mrs (widow)	Domestic duties	3 Huntscroft Gardens	
Woolven Maurice Mr	Painter's Labourer	6 Council Cottages	
Woolven Thomas Mr	Retired	7 Huntscroft Gardens	
Woolven Julia Mrs	Domestic duties	7 Huntscroft Gardens	

Name	Occupation	Residence	Comment
Woolven Thomas Mr	Carpenter and Painter	2 South Lodge Cottage, Lwr Beeding	
Woolven Grace Mrs	Domestic duties	2 South Lodge Cottage, Lwr Beeding	
Woolven Walter Mr	General Labourer	Brick Kiln Cottages, Lwr Beeding	
Woolven Katherine Mrs	Domestic duties	Brick Kiln Cottages, Lwr Beeding	
Woodman George Mr	Gardener	The Ferns, Mill Lane, Lwr Beeding	
Worsfold Frank Mr	Farmer	Goodyears Farm, Mill Lane	
Worsfold Annie Mrs	Domestic duties	Goodyears Farm, Mill Lane	
Worsfold Albert Mr	Gardener	Goodyears Farm, Mill Lane	
Worsfold William Mr	Gardener	Goodyears Farm, Mill Lane	
Worskett Annie Miss	Maid	Brookhill House	
Wren Frederick Mr	Dairy Farmer	West Ridge Farm	
Wren Annie Mrs	Domestic duties	West Ridge Farm	
Wren Leslie	At school	West Ridge Farm	
Wright Minnie Mrs	Domestic duties	3 Oakfield Cottages	Evacuee
Wright William Mr	HGV Lorry Driver	Massetts	
Wright Selina Mrs	Domestic duties	Massetts	
Yates Adeline Miss	Housemaid	Barnfield	
Yates Henry Mr	Farm Labourer	Baldwins Cottage	
Yates Elizabeth Mrs	Domestic duties	Baldwins Cottage	
Yates Mark Mr	Incapacitated	1 Rock Cottage	
Young Wilfred Mr	Horticultural Gardener	4 Mill Lane, Lwr Beeding	
Young Edith Mrs	Domestic duties	4 Mill Lane, Lwr Beeding	
Young Colin	Under school age (7 months)	4 Mill Lane, Lwr Beeding	
Young George Mr	Bricklayer (incapacitated)	4 Mill Lane, Lwr Beeding	

Appendix B

Maps of Cowfold in 1939

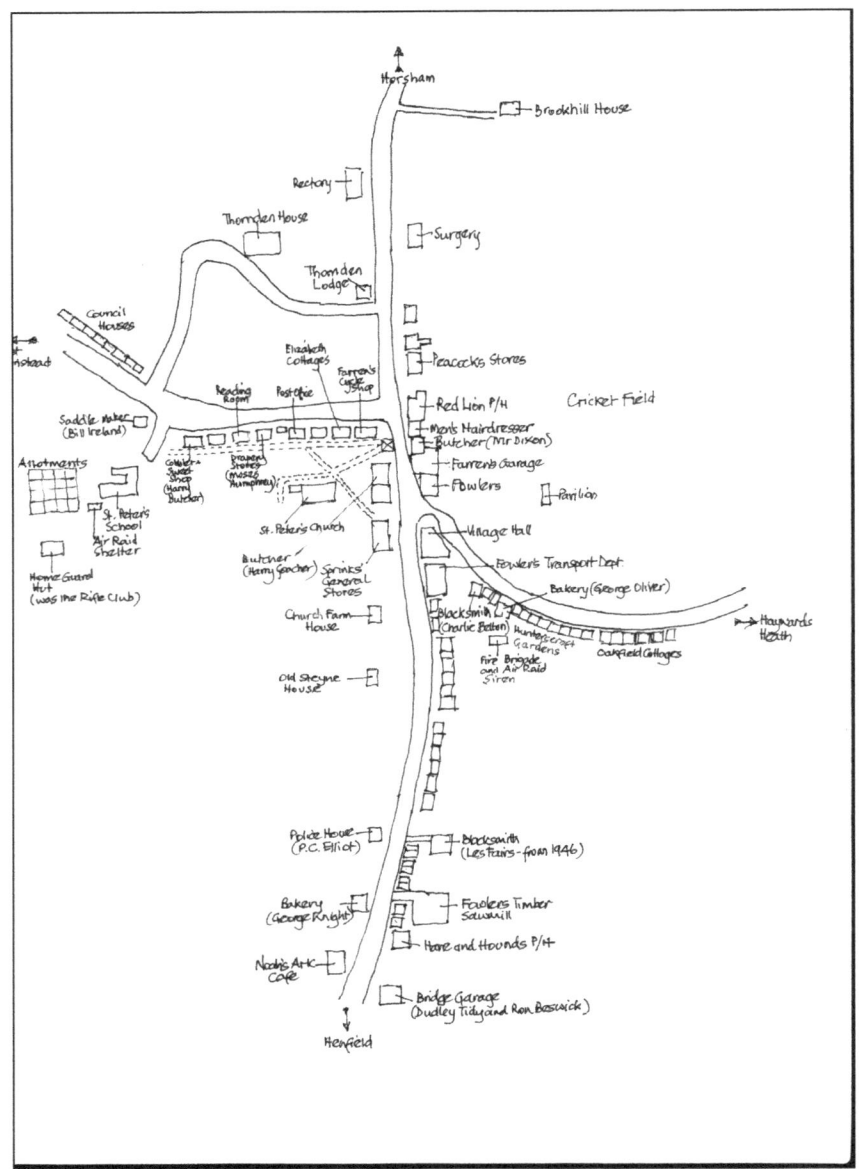

Cowfold Village 1939

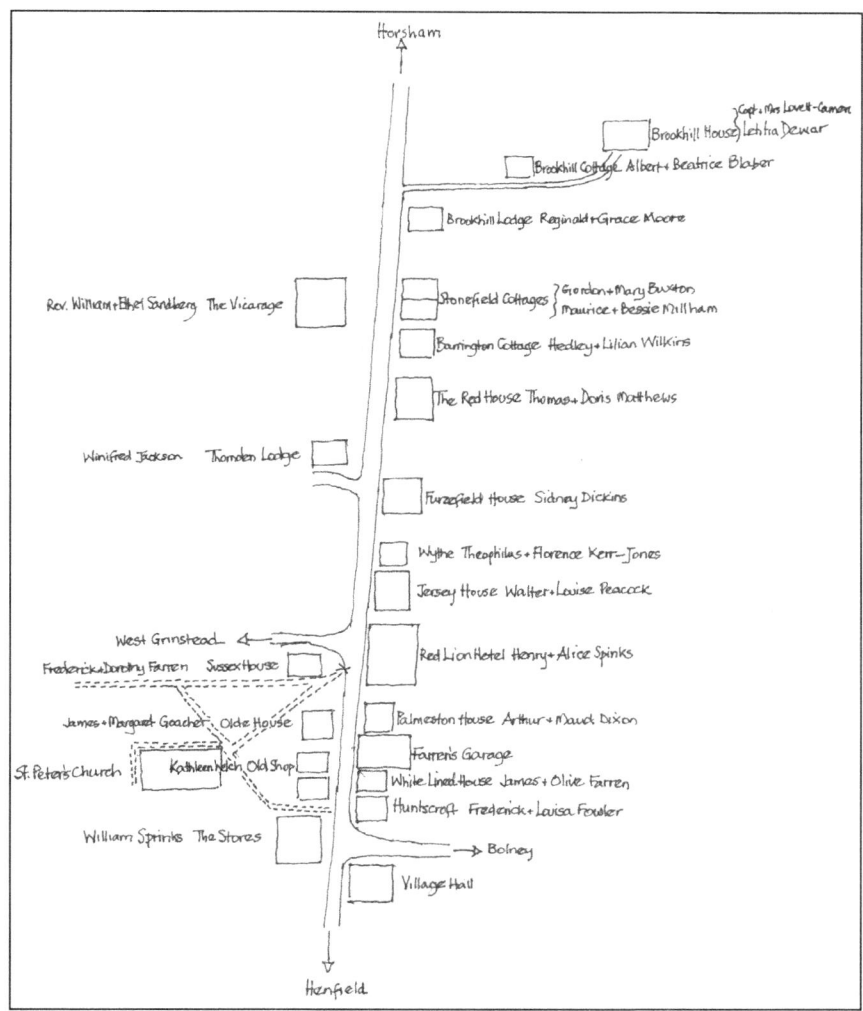

Horsham

Capt. + Mrs Lovell-Camara
Brookhill House) Lehtia Dewar
Brookhill Cottage Albert + Beatrice Blaber
Brookhill Lodge Reginald + Grace Moore
Rev. William + Ethel Sandberg   The Vicarage
Stonefield Cottages } Gordon + Mary Buxton
Maurice + Bessie Millham
Barrington Cottage Hedley + Lilian Wilkins
The Red House Thomas + Doris Matthews
Winifred Jackson   Thornden Lodge
Furzefield House Sidney Dickins
Wythe Theophilus + Florence Kerr-Jones
Jersey House Walter + Louise Peacock
West Grinstead
Frederick + Dorothy Farren   Sussex House
Red Lion Hotel Henry + Alice Spinks
James + Margaret Goacher   Olde House
Palmeston House Arthur + Maud Dixon
St. Peter's Church   Kathleen Welch Old Shop
Farren's Garage
White Lined House James + Olive Farren
Huntscroft Frederick + Louisa Fowler
William Sprinks The Stores
Bolney
Village Hall

Henfield

Cowfold Village 1939: The Street and Horsham Road

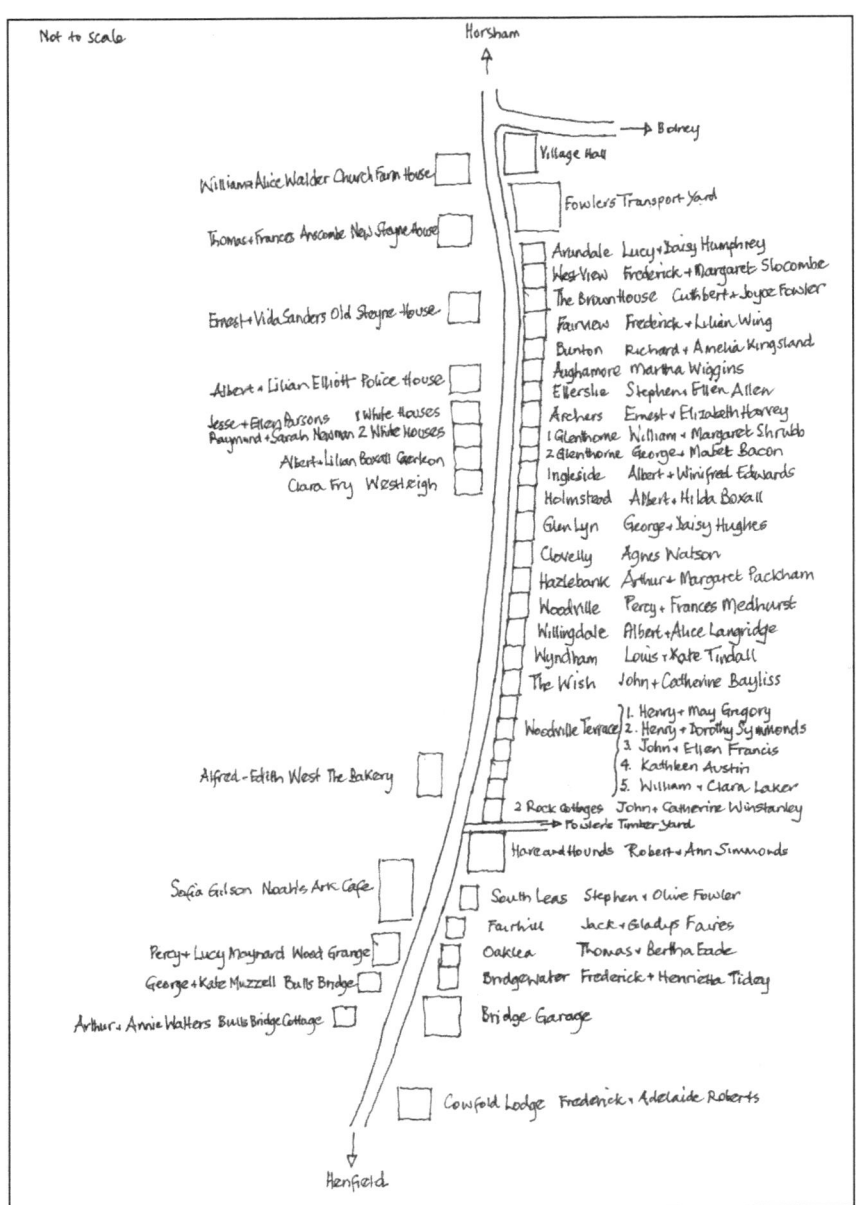

Cowfold Village 1939: Henfield Road (not to scale)

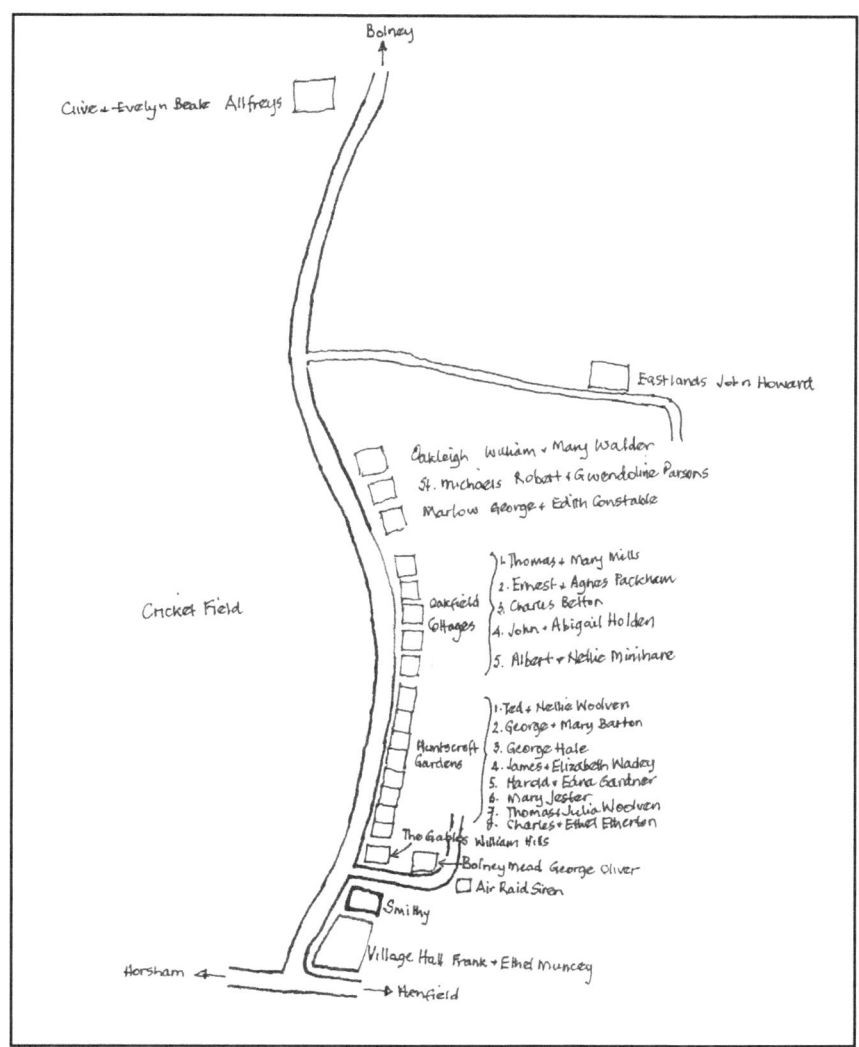

Cowfold Village 1939: Bolney Road (not to scale)

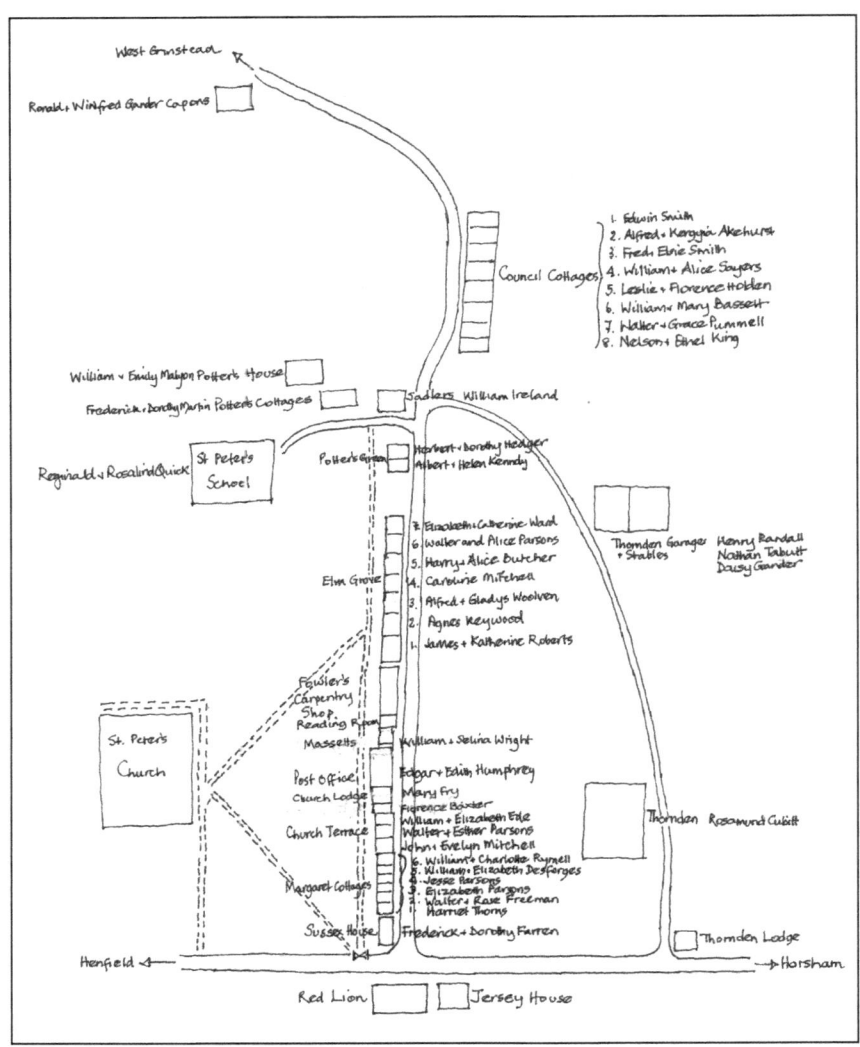

Cowfold Village 1939: Station Road (not to scale)

Appendix C

The Skies over Cowfold during WW2

Michael J. Gething, *MRAeS*

With 22 aerodromes, airfields and Advanced Landing Grounds (ALGs) scattered across the central southern area of England [see map], air activity in the skies over Cowfold would have been a regular sight during the Second World War. Some of the airfields were established RAF bases, several with designated satellite fields to disperse aircraft against enemy bomber attacks; then in 1944, as the tempo of the build-up to Operation Overlord (D-Day) increased, many ALGs were created. These were temporary airfields with minimal facilities used by fighters and fighter-bombers to support the D-Day landings.

However, throughout the war, it is likely that many types of military aircraft – fighters, bombers, transports and light observation types – operated by the Royal Air Force (RAF), many manned by crew from the Empire (now Commonwealth) and 'escaped' nationals from Occupied Europe, such as the Belgians,

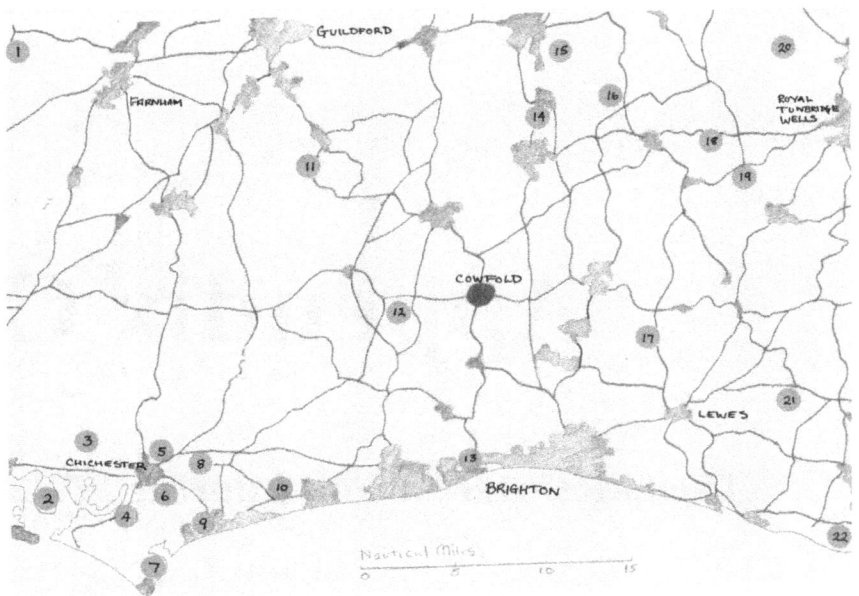

Airfields and Landing Grounds located in Central Southern England (numbered L-R from top LH corner). Source: *RAF Squadrons (2nd Edition)* – Wg Cmdr C. G. Jefford, (Airlife 2001)

1 = Odiham	12 = Coolham
2 = Thorney Island	13 = Shoreham
3 = Funtington	14 = Gatwick
4 = Appledram	15 = Redhill
5 = Westhampnett	16 = Horne
6 = Merston	17 = Chailey
7 = Selsey	18 = East Grinstead / Hammerwood Park
8 = Tangmere	19 = Hartfield
9 = Bognor	20 = Penshurst / Chiddingstone Causeway
10 = Ford / Yapton	21 = Deanland
11 = Dunsfold	22 = Friston

Czechs, Dutch, French, Norwegians and Poles), the Fleet Air Arm (FAA) and the US Army Air Force (USAAF) – could have been seen at one time or another.

That said, during the Battle of Britain (BoB) in autumn 1940, Supermarine Spitfire and Hawker Hurricane fighters were the most common types to be seen, although Bristol Blenheim fighter-bombers were not uncommon. As the war progressed, however, Bristol Beaufighters, de Havilland Mosquitos, Douglas A-20 Havocs/Bostons (both RAF and USAAF) and North American B-25 Mitchells (again RAF and USAAF) would have been in evidence. By the time Operation Overlord was approaching, later-model Spitfires, Hawker Typhoons and North American P-51 Mustangs of the RAF, together with Republic P-47 Thunderbolt and P-51 Mustang fighters, plus B-25 Mitchell bombers, of the USAAF, would also be seen. (The larger Boeing B-17 Flying Fortresses and Consolidated B-24 Liberators were based in East Anglia.) Ahead of the D-Day landings, various light aircraft, transports, troop-carrying gliders and their towing aircraft could have been visible.

Enemy aircraft, too, were likely to have been seen in the skies over England, although mostly during the first half of the war. *Luftwaffe*

An Explanation of the Aircraft Nomenclature used

The first time an aircraft type is mentioned, the manufacturer's name and aircraft name is given, sometimes with the mark number; there-after just the aircraft name and (where known) the mark number. For British aircraft, this will be in Roman numerals (e.g. IV = the Mk.IV or Mk.4), with any sub-variant (where known) designated by a lower case letter (e.g. Vb = the Mk.Vb or Mk.5b). Later in the war, role designator letter would be introduced (e.g. FB.VI = Fighter Bomber Mk.VI or Mk.6). For American aircraft, the designation precedes the name; although these are omitted where the type was used by the RAF.

types likely to have been seen were the Messerschmitt Bf.109, Messerschmitt Bf.110 and Focke Wulf Fw.190/Ta.152 fighters; and bombers such as the Dornier Do.17/Do.215/Do.217 series, Heinkel He.111, Junkers Ju.87 *Stuka* and Ju.88.

The following look at the 22 airfields/ALGs identified is intended to record the flying units based there, so as to give an indication of the spread of allied air power located around Cowfold during the war. These accounts are not presented as full histories of the sites, although some background may be given. The number in brackets is the location identification key on the map.

Appledram (4)

This ALG opened in May 1943, hosting three squadrons of Typhoon Ib (175, 181 and 182 Sqns) from 2nd June to 2nd July 1943. In April 1944, three Polish Spitfire IX units arrived (310, 312 and 312 Sqn), to be replaced in late June 1944 with three more Polish units (302, 308 and 317 Sqns) also flying Spitfire IXs, moving on in mid-July. By November 1944, Appledram had been de-commissioned.

Bognor (9)

Built as a relief landing ground for Tangmere, Bognor opened in June 1943 and for a month hosted 19 Sqn (Spitfire Vc), 122 Sqn and 602 Sqn, (both flying the Spitfire Vb). From the end of March 1944, Bognor became an ALG, with three more Spitfire units: – 66 Sqn and 331 Sqn (both with the LF.IXb model) and 332 Sqn (with a mix of Mk.Vb and Mk.IXb models). In between times, Spitfires, Mustangs and Typhoons could be seen using the airfield, as well as an ambulance-configured Avro Anson from 1310 Flight. The site was returned to agricultural use in early 1945.

Chailey (17)

Laid out in 1943 and demolishing the local pub in the process ('The

Plough' was rebuilt about half a mile away), the Chailey ALG was dedicated to supporting Operation Overlord. Between 26th April and 19th June 1944, it hosted 131 Polish Wing, comprising 302, 308 and 317 Sqns, all flying the Spitfire IX. It also acted as the base for 18 Fighter Section, controlling three wings, each of three squadrons. The airfield was de-requisitioned in 1945 and returned to farm use.

Coolham (12)

The ALG established at Coolham in 1943 was the nearest airfield to Cowfold. From April to June 1944, it hosted three Mustang III units: 129, 306 and 315 Sqns – the latter two being Polish-manned. Following their departure, three Spitfire LF.IXb units (222, 349 and 485 Sqns) moved in at the end of June for a few days, departing on 4th July 1944. While the ALG was being decommissioned, a USAAF B-24 Liberator made a forced landing on 19th January 1945 and, after repairs, flew out on 26th January.

Deanland (21)

Built as an ALG in 1943, Deanland was not activated until April 1944, although one source credits 64 Sqn as flying the Spitfire Vc from there from 2nd February to 26th June 1944. For a brief period in April 1944, it hosted 131 Polish Wing, comprising 302, 308 and 317 Sqns, all flying the Spitfire IX, plus 234 Sqn (Spitfire VI) and 611 Sqn (Spitfire LF.Vb) from April to June 1944.

On 21st July 1944, 91 Sqn arrived with the Spitfire XIV, exchanging them for the Spitfire IXb in August, before departing in October 1944. Operating alongside them was 322 Sqn, also flying the Spitfire XIV to August 1944, when it re-equipped with the Spitfire LF.IXe, departing in October 1944. When flying the Spitfire XIV (powered by the more-powerful Rolls-Royce Griffon 60-series in place of the Merlin, and therefore faster), these two units were engaged in combating the V-1 'Doodlebug' menace.

Between August and October 1944, 345 Sqn flew the Spitfire Vb from Deanland, exchanging them for the HF.IX model in September 1944. Site clearance began in November 1944 and Deanland was returned to civil use.

Dunsfold (11)

Now better known as the home of the 'Top Gear' TV show, Dunsfold was built as an ALG by the Canadian Army in 1942 and was under control of the Royal Canadian Air Force (RCAF) until 1944. The first aircraft based there were Mustang I fighters of 400, 414 and 430 Sqn, RCAF, from December 1942 to July 1943, when it reverted back to the RAF, after which it hosted 231 Sqn (Mustang I) for barely a month.

Between August 1943 and October 1944, 139 Wing were resident, flying Mitchell II medium bombers, supplemented from February-May 1944 by 320 Sqn, crewed by personnel from the Dutch Naval Aviation Service, also flying the Mitchell II. A detachment from 21 Sqn, flying Mosquito FB.VI fighter-bombers, operated from Dunsfold between April and June 1944.

Following 139 Wing came the 83 Group Support Unit in the autumn of 1944, with a variety of Spitfire, Typhoon and Hawker Tempest aircraft: 276 Sqn, flying the Spitfire Vb, disbanded at Dunsfold in November 1945, and afterwards the airfield was used to repatriate prisoners-of-war until declared inactive in 1946.

East Grinstead / Hammerwood Park (18)

Located in Hammerwood Park, this simple airstrip (not even up to ALG standards) hosted 660 Sqn from 20th November 1943 to 23rd April 1944, flying Taylorcraft Auster III air observation post (AOP) light aircraft, changing to the improved Mk.IV model in February 1944. It was joined by 659 Sqn (Auster IV) from 23rd April to 14th June 1944. Today it is a private helicopter landing pad.

Ford / Yapton (10)

Originally operated as a military airfield from March 1918 to 1920 (when it was known as Ford Junction), the airfield at Ford (also known as Yapton) was used for civil flying in the mid-1930s and resumed military use in 1937, when the FAA based training units there. Following a devastating attack by Ju.87 *Stukas* in August 1940, the RAF deployed to Ford, with its first unit, 23 Sqn, arriving in September 1940. Initially flying the Blenheim If (the fighter variant of the light bomber with an under-fuselage gun pack containing four 0.303in machine guns), the squadron pioneered Intruder operations (roaming enemy-occupied territory to attack targets at will). Re-equipping with the Havoc I, then the Boston III, it achieved considerable success. By the time 23 Sqn departed in September 1942, it was flying the Mosquito NF.II.

A detachment of 107 Sqn (Blenheim IV) arrived at Ford in May 1941, staying until August 1943; while a detachment from 43 Sqn (Hurricane IIb) flew from October 1941 to June 1942, supplemented by a detachment of 174 Sqn (also with the Hurricane IIb) between March and July 1942. Between July 1942 and March 1943, another Intruder unit, 605 Sqn (flying Havoc I, Boston III and Mosquito NF.II over time) was based there; supplemented by a detachment of Boston III aircraft from 88 Sqn, September 1942 to March 1943.

In August 1942, 141 Sqn arrived at Ford, flying the Beaufighter If, departing in February 1943, followed by 604 Sqn (also Beaufighter If) between February and April 1943. A third Beaufighter If unit, 256 Sqn, arrived in April 1943, re-equipping with the Mosquito XIII in May, before departing in August 1943. During February and March 1943, the airfield briefly hosted 16 and 170 Sqns, flying the Spitfire V and Mustang I fighters, respectively; with 418 Sqn (Mosquito NF.II) arriving during March 1943 (until April 1944). Spitfire LF.Vb fighters of 611 Sqn made a brief deployment in November 1943.

September 1943 had seen 29 Sqn arrive with its Mosquito FB.VI fighter-bombers, re-equipping with the Mosquito XIII during their sojourn at Ford, ending in March 1944; followed by 456 Sqn with Mosquito XVII aircraft between February and December 1944, with 96 Sqn (Mosquito XIII) joining them on Intruder operations between June and September.

There was much fighter-bomber activity in 1944, ahead of and after D-Day: a wing of Mustang III aircraft (19, 44 and 122 Sqns) operated from Ford between April and May; followed in June/July by 129, 306 and 315 Sqns, also with the Mustang III. Ford also hosted a wing of Spitfire IXb aircraft between April and May, comprising 132, 453 and 602 Sqns, followed in May by an Australian wing (441, 442 and 443 Sqns) also flying the Spitfire IXb, which departed in June.

Between July and August 1944, 131 Polish Wing (302, 308 and 317 Sqns) flew the Spitfire IX from Ford; while other Spitfire units briefly rotated through in August – 66 and 331 Sqns flying the LF.IXb, model, 127 Sqn (LF.IXe) and 332 Sqn with the Mk.Vb. By 1945, with the war in Europe approaching the 'end game', Ford reverted back to the FAA (hosting various trials units), finally closing as a military site in 1958.

Friston (22)

Created as an Emergency Landing Ground from a private airstrip at Gayles Farm (near Cuckfield Haven) in 1940, Friston was further developed as a fighter airfield over the winter of 1941/42, receiving its first units – 32 and 253 Sqns (both flying the Hurricane I) – in June 1942, finally departing in August 1942. Between May and June 1943, 41Sqn (Spitfire XII) deployed to Friston, supplemented by 412 Sqn (Spitfire Vb) in June/July, and 64 Sqn (Spitfire Vb) in August 1943, 306 Sqn (Spitfire Vb) during August/September and 308 Sqn (Spitfire Vb) in September 1943.

From November 1943 to March 1944, 349 Sqn (Spitfire Vc) was in residence, converting to the Spitfire LF.IXe in February 1944, ahead of its onwards move. March/April saw the return of 41 Sqn, which re-appeared briefly in July. Between April and July, 501Sqn (Spitfire IX) flew from Friston, followed by 316 (Polish) Sqn with the Mustang III for a few weeks in July/August 1944. Between July and September, 610 Sqn with the Griffon-engined Spitfire XIV was operational, supplemented by 131 Sqn (Spitfire VII) from August to November 1944. These units were employed in the battle against the V-1 'Doodlebug' flying bombs from June to September, with 316 Sqn recording 75 'kills' during its deployment. The final unit to be based at Friston was 666 Sqn (Auster V) between April and May 1945, when it departed for the Netherlands.

Throughout the war, Friston's role as an emergency landing ground continued, with aircraft as big as the RAF's Avro Lancaster and the USAAF B-17 Flying Fortress landing safely there. It ceased to be used as an airfield from October 1944 and was de-commissioned in April 1946.

Funtington (3)

Rated as one of the busiest ALGs in operation 1943-1944, Funtington hosted many units and aircraft types, as it was RAF policy to move squadrons around the ALGs so as not to present a static target. Mustang I army co-operation fighters of 2 and 268 Sqns, RAF, flew from Funtington in September/October 1943, followed by several RCAF squadrons flying Spitfire IXs (441, 442 and 443 Sqns) and Typhoons (438, 439 and 440 Sqns) during April 1944.

April/May 1944 saw Funtington host 65 and 122 Sqns, flying Mustang IIIs, followed between 17-22 June (post the D-Day landings) by 164, 183, 198 and 609 Sqns operating the Typhoon Ib on ground attack duties. June/July saw 329, 340 and 341 Sqns operating Spitfire IXs, after which 222, 349 and 485 Sqns (the latter being RNZAF-manned) took over, also flying Spitfire IXs. Between 6-8 August, 66, 127, 331 and 332 Sqns (the latter two units having Norwegian pilots) flew Spitfire IXs from Funtington. By December 1944, the ALG had been returned to agricultural use.

Gatwick (14)

Originally known as Lowfield Heath aerodrome in the late-1920s, commercial flights from Gatwick began in 1933, with its first terminal building ('The Beehive') constructed in 1935. Taken over by the RAF, a detachment from 98 Sqn (flying the Blenheim If) arriving in December 1939 until May 1940, when 18 and 57 Sqns arrived with the Blenheim IV (departing in June 1940) and, operating briefly in June/July, 53 Sqn (also the Blenheim IV) and 98 Sqn flying the (by-then obsolete) Fairey Battle light bomber.

September 1940 saw the arrival of 239 Sqn with the Westland Lysander II/III army co-operation aircraft (until July 1941) with Boulton-Paul Defiant I fighters of 141 Sqn operating during October and November 1940. Between May 1941 and November 1942, detachments from 309 Sqn (initially with the Lysander IIIa and, from August 1942, the Mustang I) were deployed to Gatwick, as were detachments from 400 Sqn, flying a mix of Curtiss P-40 Tomahawk I/IIa/IIb fighters between June 1941 and June 1942. More brief detachments from 2 and 26 Sqns (initially flying the Tomahawk II, then in 1942, the Mustang I) flew between July 1941 and January 1943.

May 1942 saw the arrival of several Mustang I units: the first being 239 Sqn (until August 1942, returning briefly in April to June 1943), followed by 63 Sqn (June-July), 613 Sqn (August 1942 to March 1943) and 171Sqn (September to December). Between August and September 1942, Gatwick also hosted 116 Sqn, flying Airspeed Oxford II trainers. Hurricane IIb fighters of 175 Sqn were also based here between December 1942 and January 1943.

The lightweight Auster III AOP aircraft of 655 Sqn were briefly based at Gatwick during March and April 1943, as were the Typhoon Ib ground attack fighters of 183 Sqn (April-May 1943). More Mustang I fighters from 414 and 430 Sqns rotated through the airfield between July 1943 and April 1944; while 19 and 65 Sqns (Spitfire IX) used Gatwick in October 1943.

March 1944 saw a brief deployment from 168 Sqn (Mustang I), with 268 Sqn (with the Mustang Ia) resident in April/May. Also during April, 4 Sqn (Spitfire XI) arrived, departing in June; only to be replaced by a wing of Spitfire IX fighters (80, 229 and 274 Sqns), June-July 1944. Between August 1944 and January 1945, 287 Sqn operated from Gatwick, initially with the Spitfire Vb then, from September 1944 with the Beaufighter VI, and from November 1944, with the Spitfire IX and Tempest V. To wrap the year, between August and October 1945, 14 Sqn, flying the Mosquito FB.VI was based there.

After the war, the site (extending northwards) was re-developed into London's second international airport, re-opening in 1958.

Hartfield (19)

Located some 2.5 miles east-south-east of Hammerwood Park (see East Grinstead / Hammerwood Park), this simple airstrip (probably just a farmer's field in the vicinity of Hartfield village) briefly hosted 658 Sqn, flying the Auster IV AOP light aircraft, from 19 April to 25 June 1944. [Nothing else can be found regarding this 'airfield'.]

Horne (16)

Constructed in three months, Horne ALG was used by three units for just seven weeks from 30th April to 19th June 1944. The site hosted 130 Sqn (Spitfire Vb), 303 (Polish) Sqn (with the low-level Spitfire LF.Vb) and 402 (Canadian) Sqn (Spitfire Vc). Thereafter, it served as a barrage balloon site (defending again the V-1 'Doodlebug' menace) for a month and was returned to farmland in 1945.

Merston (6)

Built between 1939 and 1941, Merston was initially another satellite of RAF Tangmere, with145 Sqn (Spitfire IIb) operating there from May to July 1941 and 41 Sqn (Spitfire Vb) from April to June 1942. Then handed-over to the US Eighth Air Force as a satellite of Westhampnett, it became home to the 307th Fighter Squadron (of the USAAF's 31st Fighter Group) operating Spitfire Vbs (supplied under a reverse 'Lend/Lease' arrangement) between August and October 1942.

After some redevelopment, it reverted to the RAF in May 1943 and saw many units rotate through (some for just a matter of days). Among those identified are 485 (New Zealand) Sqn (Spitfire Vb) May to July 1943, 402 (Canadian) Sqn (Spitfire Vc) August/September 1943 and 303 (Polish) Sqn (Spitfire LF.Vb) June to August 1944. Merston was finally closed in 1945.

Odiham (1)

Opened as a permanent base in 1937, Odiham was the furthest away from Cowfold. During the war, it hosted RAF units (again too many to list individually) flying the Mustang Mks I, II and IV, Spitfire XI, Blenheim IV, Lysander III and Mosquito XIII. After D-Day, the site was used to house enemy Prisoners-of-War. Today it is the home of the RAF's Chinook helicopter fleet.

Penshurst / Chiddingstone Causeway (20)

Opened in 1916 and used during the First World War, the airfield at Penshurst hosted civil aircraft until 1936. Re-occupied by the RAF as an Emergency Landing Ground, between March and June 1940, it was used by 15 Elementary Flying Training School at Redhill as a relief landing ground.

On 27th October 1940, a Messerschmitt Bf.109E made a wheels-up landing at Penshurst, followed by the Spitfire IIa (of 74 Sqn) which shot it down. The two pilots apparently engaged in a fist-fight, broken up by an ARP Warden and policeman! From 4th to 8th August 1941, Tomahawk IIa army co-operation fighters of 268 Sqn operated briefly from the site.

From September 1942 to 17 August 1943, the base hosted 653 Sqn flying the Auster V AOP aircraft but the unit returned again on 17 September 1943, finally departing on 27th June 1944. It was immediately replaced by 661 Sqn (with the Auster IV), which departed to the Netherlands on 7th August 1944.

On 6th July 1944, a B-17 Flying Fortress of the 603rd Bombardment Squadron, USAAF made an emergency wheels-up landing at Penshurst. The aircraft was later repaired and flown out with a light load and taking advantage of favourable winds.

The final flying unit to be based at Penshurst was 664 Sqn, flying the Auster V, between 2nd February and 23rd March 1945. On 10th July 1945, a C-47A Dakota transport assigned to the 23rd Fighter Squadron, USAAF, crashed on landing at Penshurst, and was written off. The base was closed on 13th May 1946

Redhill (15)

Initially in use as a private airfield in the 1920s, Redhill's use expanded in the 1930s and, in July 1937, housed an 15 Elementary Flying Training School (EFTS) flying Miles Magister trainers and Fairey Battle light bombers. October 1939 saw a detachment from 219 Sqn, flying the Blenheim If, make a brief deployment; then, in June 1940, under threat of German attack, the EFTS moved north and the airfield became an operational RAF station.

The first unit to arrive was 16 Sqn (Lysander I) in June 1940, but moved on before the month's end. This was to be a pattern at Redhill – short deployments of mainly fighter units. In September 1940, 219 Sqn returned, this time flying the Beaufighter If, departing during December. A Hurricane IIb unit, 1 Sqn, operated from May to July 1941, supplemented during June by 258 Sqn (Hurricane IIa).

The first Spitfires arrived in April 1942 with 340 Sqn, flying the Mk.Vb, moving on before the end of the month; followed briefly in July by 308 Sqn (Mk.IIa) and 310 Sqn (Mk.Vb). Two more Spitfire Vb units arrived in July: 312 Sqn staying until August and 350 Sqn, staying until September; while a third Mk.Vb unit (303 Sqn) also spent time at Redhill in August. August 1943 saw the brief deployment of 66 Sqn, flying the high-altitude Spitfire VI, and 131 Sqn (Spitfire Vc), which departed the following month.

Between October 1943 and January 1944, Redhill hosted 231 Sqn, flying the Mustang 1, with the last fighter unit, 287 Sqn, operating the Tempest V between November 1944 and January 1945. A non-operational unit, 116 Sqn, flying the Oxford II and Anson XII, was based at Redhill between September 1944 and March 1945. The airfield returned to civil use in 1947 and is still used today.

Selsey (7)

Initially a private airstrip before the war, Selsey was developed as an ALG from 1941, with the first unit, 65 Sqn (Spitfire V) arriving on 31st May 1943, followed by 245 Sqn (Typhoon Ib) a day later. Both squadrons stayed just one month. April 1944 saw the arrival of 349 Sqn and 485 (New Zealand) Sqn, both flying the Spitfire LF.IXe, staying until the end of June, plus 222 Sqn (Spitfire LF.IXb) which stayed but a few days.

July 1944 saw 74 Sqn (Spitfire LF.IXe) reside for a few days. Then later 329 Sqn (Spitfire IX) made a brief appearance, to be followed by 340 Sqn and 341 Sqn (both flying the Spitfire LF.IXb) through to August. These units were followed by 33 Sqn (Spitfire LF.IXe) and 222 Sqn (Spitfire LF.IXb) for a brief period. Thereafter Selsey reverted to a reserve airfield and closed in March 1945.

Shoreham (13)

Flying commenced from at site at Shoreham in 1910 and, during the First World War, it was used for training by the Royal Flying Corps. In 1930 the municipal authorities of Brighton, Hove and Worthing established Shoreham as the municipal airport for all three towns and it was officially opened on the 13th June, 1936. Following the German invasion of France in 1940, all civil flying from Shoreham ceased.

After a short break, the RAF moved in with a detachment from 225 Sqn flying the Lysander II/III from July 1940 to July 1941. In December, a detachment of 277 Sqn operated in the air-sea rescue role with Supermarine Walrus amphibian biplanes until December 1942, being involved in the rescue of nearly 600 airmen from the Channel.

A detachment of Hurricane IIc fighters from 3 Sqn operated from Shoreham from June 1941, swapping them for the Typhoon Ib in February 1943 before moving on in May. Another detachment from 245 Sqn (flying the Hurricane IIb/c) operated between December 1941 and October 1942, supplemented for a few days in May 1942 by 253 Sqn (with the Hurricane IIa). Two squadrons of Spitfire Vb fighters (277 and 345 Sqns) operated in support of the D-Day landings from April to October 1944.

One other unit, a detachment of 667 Sqn, is recorded as operating from Shoreham between December 1943 and December 1945, flying a variety of aircraft including the Defiant I/II, Hurricane IIc, Fairey Barracuda II, Oxford, Vultee Vengence IV and the Spitfire XVI.

During the war, Shoreham was the target of several air raids. In one attack, the outer skin of the main hangar was blown off but the Art Deco terminal building remaining undamaged throughout. The airfield returned to civil flying in 1946.

Tangmere (8)

Established in 1917, Tangmere was used through 1918, re-opening in 1925 and re-developed in 1939 to defend the south coast. During the course of the war, over 80 RAF and allied squadrons were based there, too many to record in detail. The following offers representative snapshots of units and aircraft based there.

At the outbreak of war on 3rd September 1939, the resident units were 1 and 43 Sqns, both flying the Hurricane I were in situ but 1 Sqn departed to France within days as part of the air component of the British Expeditionary Force. August 1940 saw a detachment from 1 Sqn return until early September. 43 Sqn remained at Tangmere until November 1939, but returned in May 1940 until September. In October 1939, 92 Sqn reformed there on the Blenheim If before moving on at the end of December 1939. November 1939 also saw the arrival of 501 Sqn (Hurricane I), staying until May 1940.

By then, ahead of the Battle of Britain, 145 Sqn arrived at Tangmere, joined in June by 601 Sqn, and (briefly) in mid-August by 17 Sqn, all flying the Hurricane I. From October 1940 to June 1942, 219 Sqn (Beaufighter If) was based there, later joined briefly by 141 Sqn (also Beaufighter If) in June to August 1942. Between November 1940 and February 1941, 65 Sqn (initially on the Spitfire I, then the Mk.IIa) flew from Tangmere.

March 1941 saw 145, 610 and 616 Sqns, equipped with the cannon-armed Spitfire Vb, led by newly-promoted Wing Commander Douglas Bader (who preferred to fly the Spitfire Va armed with eight 0.303in machine guns) operate from Tangmere. On 9th August 1941, Bader was forced to bail out (most recent theories suggest a victim of 'friendly fire') over France and was taken prisoner. (His story is told in Paul Brickhill's book, *Reach for the Sky*, subsequently filmed with Kenneth More as Bader.)

June 1942 saw 43 Sqn return to Tangmere, flying the Hurricane IIc, moving again on 1 September. The next month, 486 (New

Zealand) Sqn arrived with its Typhoon Ib, which it exchanged for the Tempest V in January 1944 ahead of another move. April 1944 saw a Canadian Wing of Spitfire IXb fighters (401, 411 and 412 Sqns) arrive for Operation Overlord, remaining until mid-June 1944. A single unit, 331 (Norwegian) Sqn, equipped with the Spitfire IXb) flew from Tangmere between June and August 1944. In November 1944, 26 Sqn made a brief deployment to Tangmere. Initially flying the Hurricane IIc, the unit re-equipped with the Mustang I then departed in early December.

Between February 1942 and June 1945, Tangmere periodically played host to 161 (Special Duties) Sqn, whose Lysander IIIa and Lockheed Hudson I aircraft were used for insertion and recovery operations into Occupied France for the Special Operations Executive.

Tangmere continued as an operational RAF airfield until closure in 1970.

Thorney Island (2)

Built in 1938 as a fighter base, it was active during the BoB, hosting 236 Sqn flying Blenheim If fighters for a short time, and was attacked by the *Luftwaffe*. Transferred to Coastal Command, concrete runways were laid in 1942, enabling it to operate larger four-engined general reconnaissance aircraft used by the RAF for maritime surveillance, including the Flying Fortress (59 Sqn) and Liberator III (53, 59 and 86 Sqns).

Throughout the war, Thorney Island hosted many units of both the RAF and FAA (again, too many to list individually), flying a variety of types which (in addition to the ones mentioned above) included Anson, Grumman Avenger, Barracuda, Blenheim, Bristol Beaufort, Beaufighter, Handley Page Hampden, Hudson, Mosquito, Spitfire, Fairey Swordfish, Vickers Wellington, Armstrong Whitworth Whitley and, during Operation Overlord, Typhoon Ib aircraft.

The airfield continued as an RAF station after the war, closing in 1976 and was later taken-over by the Royal Artillery.

Westhampnett (5)

Created on the Goodwood Estate, Westhampnett operated as a satellite airfield to Tangmere, being operational from July 1940 to May 1946, seeing many units rotated through as the war progressed. During the summer of 1940, 43 and 145 Sqns (both Hurricane I) operated from there, followed by 602 Sqn (Spitfire I) to December 1940. Between November 1940 and May 1941, 302 (Polish) Sqn (Hurricane I, later IIa) were based at Westhampnett while, during late 1941, 65 Sqn (Spitfire II, later Vb) were in situ. From December 1941, 41 Sqn (Spitfire Vb) were on site until April 1942, as was 129 Sqn (Spitfire Vb).

From August to October 1942, the USAAF's 309th Fighter Squadron operated Spitfire Vbs from the base, followed by 616 Sqn flying the high altitude Spitfire VI from October through to January 1943. They were followed by 610 Sqn (Spitfire Vc), then 501 Sqn (Spitfire Vc, later the Mk.IX) flying there from April to June. The run-up to D-Day saw Spitfire IXbs of 443 (Canadian) Sqn deploy to Tangmere in April 1944, with 402 (Canadian) Sqn (Spitfire Vc) and 303 (Polish) Sqn (Spitfire LF.Vb) both operating briefly during June, with 303 Sqn returning with the Spitfire IXc in August/September 1944.

After the war, Tangmere reverted to civil use, and later had a motor racing circuit build around its perimeter, but maintaining a grass airstrip still used today.

Sources: *RAF Squadrons* by Wing Commander C. G. Jefford, *MBE, BA, RAF(Ret'd)* (Airlife Publishing, 2nd Edition 2001); *Ninety Days to Normandy* by Ken Davies (Niche Publications, 1992); plus various websites, including www.ukairfieldguide.net.

Appendix D

Wartime Recipes

Wartime Rations

Issued by the Ministry of Food (9ᵗʰ November 1939)

The following listing is for one adult (children receive half) per week

- Bacon and ham (3-4 slices/rashers) 4 oz
- Other meats – 2 small chops
- Butter 2 oz
- Cheese 2 oz
- Margarine 4 oz
- Cooking fat 4 oz
- Milk 3 pints
- Plus 1 packet dried milk per month
- Sugar 8 oz
- Preserves every two months 1 lb
- Tea 2 oz
- Egg (shell egg) 1
- Plus 1 packet dried egg per month
- Sweets 12 oz

Other foods such as canned meat, fish, rice, canned fruit, condensed milk, breakfast cereals, biscuits and vegetables were available in limited quantities on a points system. An adult's monthly allowance might provide a tin of salmon or fruit, and half a pound of dried fruit. Bread, flour, fish (if available), offal, game (including rabbit, venison, etc), sauces and pickles were not rationed, but were not always available.

Lord Woolton Pie

1lb cauliflower
1lb parsnips
1lb carrots
1lb potatoes
Bunch of spring onions chopped
2 teaspoons of Marmite (yeast extract – or you can use a
stock cube)
Tablespoon of rolled oats
Salt and pepper to taste once cooked.
Parsley (fresh or dried)

For the pastry
8oz wholemeal/wholewheat flour
4oz mashed potato
3oz margarine or lard
2 tsp of baking powder
couple large pinches of salt
Dash of water if needed.

Method
Chop up the vegetables into chunks with those that take longest to
cook into smaller pieces.

Place in pot and bring to simmer with just enough water to reach 3/4 of the way up the veg in the pot.

Add in Marmite and rolled oats, salt and pepper and cook until tender and most of the water has been absorbed.

Place mixture in deep pie dish and sprinkle with fresh parsley (or add dry parsley to mixture and mix in)

Make the pastry by mixing the flour with the baking powder and salt and then rubbing in the margarine.

Mix the mashed potato in to form a dough and knead (add a little water to the mixture if too dry)

Roll out to form pie crust and place on top and decorate then brush with milk.

Place in oven at 200C for 30 minutes or so until top is form and browned.

Cheese Frizzles

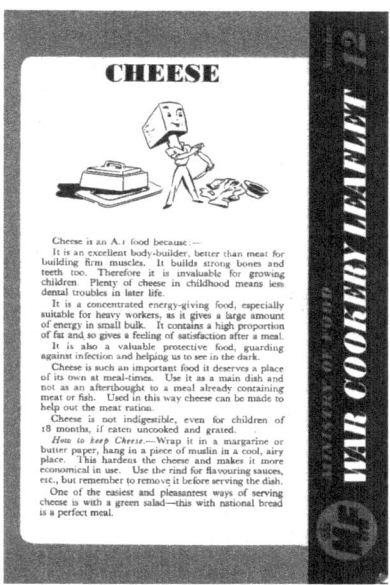

2 Tablespoons medium or coarse oatmeal.

1 Tablespoon flour.

2 Tablespoons grated cheese.

1 Teaspoon baking powder.

Salt and pepper.

A little water to mix.

Fat for frying.

Method

Mix all dry ingredients together with the exception of the baking powder, then add enough cold water to mix into a stiff batter. Just before using add the baking powder. Melt a little fat in a frying pan and when smoking hot drop spoonfuls of the mixture into hot fat. Fry till golden brown on both sides.

Potato Soup

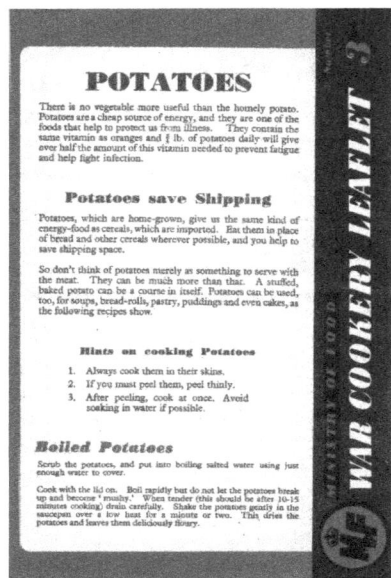

1½ lb potatoes.
1 stick celery, a few spring onions, or a little leek.
2 tablespoonfuls chopped parsley.
1¾ pints of vegetable water or water.
1 teacup of milk or household milk.
Seasoning.

Method

Scrub and slice the potatoes and celery. Place in boiling salted water. Cook with the lid on until quite soft. Rub through a sieve or mash well with a wooden spoon. Add milk and re-heat, but do not re-boil. Sprinkle in coarsely chopped parsley just before serving.

Prune Sponge

8 oz. Flour

1 oz. Fat

1 tablespoon syrup

½ teaspoon mixed spice

½ teaspoon nutmeg

½ teaspoon bicarbonate of soda

Salt

Water or milk to mix

8-12 prunes

Method

Rub the fat into the dry ingredients and mix to a soft consistency with syrup and milk or water. Place the soaked stoned prunes in the bottom of a greased basin, and pile the pudding mixture on top. Cover with a greased paper and steam for 1 ½-2 hours. Use the prune juice thickened with cornflour or custard powder as a sauce.